Dancing Naked

in Front of the Fridge

Dancing Naked

In Front
of the
Fridge

And Other Lessons from Twins

Nancy J. Sipes, Ph.D. and Janna S. Sipes, J.D.

A FairWinds Book

Dancing Naked in Front of the Fridge
By Nancy J. Sipes, Ph.D. and Janna S. Sipes, J.D
A FairWinds Book

Editing and text design: Downey Editorial Services
Cover design: Ronny Malia Anderson
Back cover photo: Susan Robertson

Published in Canada
FairWinds Press
Vancouver, B.C. Canada

Printed and bound in the United States of America

Cataloging-in-Publication Data

Sipes, Nancy J., (Nancy Jo), 1957-
    Dancing naked in front of the fridge : and other lessons from twins
ISBN 0-9682149-2-4
    1. Twins I. Sipes, Janna S., (Janna Sue) 1957- II. Title.

BF723.T9S56 1998   306.875   C98-900596-8

Dedication

To our mom, whose love, courage, and support have provided the inspiration we needed to passionately pursue our dreams. She is our soul teacher.

Also, to our dad, whose ageless wisdom played an unforgettable role in our lives. Though his time with us was short, his impact on us will never die.

Contents

Reflections

Our journey has been incredible. But we haven't made it alone. It is with grateful hearts that we reflect back on the people who have touched our lives to help make this book a reality.

Seventeen sets of very special twins, as well as many twins who casually crossed our paths, provided intimate and entertaining information about living life as twins. We are eternally thankful to them for their courage and unselfish willingness to give so that we could all learn more—about twins and relationships. Without their help, this book would not have been possible.

As we moved forward, seeking guidance on our voyage, we were blessed to meet the right teachers at the right time. Our heartfelt thanks go out to Dr. Roger Frantz, who taught us the power of our own intuition and the joy that comes from trusting it. To Mike and Tom Foley, who recognized our gifts long before we did and who have become the brothers we never had. To Ronny Anderson, who brought her creative genius to our project. To Fran Dancing Feather, who looked into our eyes, touched our souls, and spoke words to help us find our closing message. To Lauren Purcell, who shared the enthusiasm for our dreams and who has become our east-coast sister.

For Lianne and Joseph Downey, we have infinite appreciation. Throughout this venture, they gave unselfishly of themselves. Their editorial skills, words of wisdom, and visionary insights showed their love for us and our work. When we thought we had nothing left to say, they inspired us to reach inside for more. We can't thank them enough for blazing the trail ahead of us.

Our sincere thanks to Leslie Nolin at FairWinds Press. She saw a path for our book that we had not envisioned. Her patience, hard work, and endless support have made our experience not only rewarding, but also fun. A few months ago we called her our publisher; now we also call her our friend.

We could not have made this pilgrimage without the love and trust of our family and friends. None of this would have happened without our mom. We thank her for delivering us into this limitless life. Thanks to our stepfather, Earl, for being there for us for over twenty years. His courage and wisdom have often lit our path. Our sister, Brenda, her husband, Bruce, and our nephew, Kyle, have supplied hugs and love along the way. We also appreciate Brenda's walk with us down memory lane. She helped fill in the blanks to our family tales. To our niece, Joslyn, who has always been able to tell us apart (even our voices), thanks for keeping us young!

In addition, we want to give particular thanks to a mom and dad who joined our bandwagon through marriage, Nancy's in-laws, Rae and Ruby. We thank them for being true believers.

We were amazingly blessed with a dream team of friends who loved us through the laughter and the tears. They have given their time to read drafts of our manuscript and have given their hearts to elevate our dream. To Theresa, Bev, Susan, Becky, and Kay, thanks for everything. To Franklin, thank you for your quiet belief in our flight. You taught us the value of nonjudgment.

To Nancy's husband, Stu . . . we can't seem to come up with the right words to adequately thank you for your contributions. Your decision to marry into this twinship was a brave one, but you have shown even greater courage by allowing us space for creativity and by learning to accept our twin bond. You have become our biggest fan and best critic, often challenging us with your quick wit and thoughtful edits. Thanks for being a vital part of our eternal triangle. We love you.

More air beneath our wings was provided by the unconditional doggie love of Pucci, Nate, Ozzie, Search, Eddie, and Lola. Wagging tails and wet noses always brought smiles when we needed them the most.

Yes, our journey has been incredible. Yet, we know

it's not over. As it continues, we see that we now have more love than when we began. The universe has once again worked its magic and left us with hearts filled with gratitude. Our thanks to all.

INTRODUCTION
(How and Why To Dance Naked)

C hildren love to dance. Music has a magical effect on their spirits. It doesn't matter where they are, when they hear a tune, they simply can't contain themselves. Their excitement spurts out in wiggles and wild gyrations. All parts of their little bodies get into the action—heads bob, feet tap, arms swing, and joy explodes all over those who are lucky enough to witness the event. For us, as identical twins, a ready-and-willing dance partner was always available when those moments arose.

A child's dance is really an invitation for everyone to join in their celebration of life. We discovered this truth when we were about four years old. The year was 1961.

If you remember back to those days, kitchens were alive with rich and eye-catching colors. Lime green, autumn gold, and metallic copper were often the rage. The kitchen of our childhood was no exception. The walls were adorned with red, rose-patterned wallpaper, while the appliances were fashionably (okay, for *those* times!) copper-colored.

In particular, the refrigerator was brilliantly shiny and held a great fascination for us. We loved to stare at ourselves in its giant face—learning quickly, however, to simply look at, and not to touch, the reflections we saw there. Our mom had plenty to say about the million tiny fingerprints we left behind if we felt and loved our mirrored selves too much.

One morning as the family was busily getting ready to face the day, we noticed that Nancy was out of sight. (This was an unusual occurrence, since twins are generally found with one another, especially in their younger years.) The search led us to the kitchen where we found her stark naked, dancing merrily in front of that mirror-like refrigerator, gleefully admiring her wiggling, shining image. Nancy did not require music for this recital because children have the freedom to dance to their own drummer. As we stood and watched, we could almost hear the music in her head. At that moment, Nancy unashamedly earned the nickname "Dancin' Nanc" which she still carries proudly to this day.

That act of dancing naked in front of the fridge has become an inspirational metaphor for our lives. First of all, having a twin is like a continuous dance in front of a mirror. You can see yourself in the eyes of your twin, and vice versa.

But also, this symbol represents the freedom to

love yourself as an individual and to openly express your real self through your unique dance of life. The added bonus is that you end up spreading those good feelings around to others during your celebration.

This book is about celebrating life—specifically, life lived as twins. However, the lessons that appear here are not only for twins, but also for anyone who knows twins, and for all who wish to cherish and improve their human relationships.

TWINSHIP:
A MIRROR FOR ALL RELATIONSHIPS

For us, being a twin is essentially a life purpose. We believe that our existence on this earth as twins has a noble meaning. As summarized by 80-something-year-old identical twin Esther, "We always say that being twins has been a wonderful experience and blessing, and we thank God for it."

In our book, we show you how twins view their lives, and how their lives as twins flavor the world around them. Stories about their real-life adventures, as well as many of our own, illustrate and illuminate how twinships and other close relationships can be strengthened and enhanced.

We spent more than six years researching and writing these stories. Our informal work involved discussing twin life with many sets of twins. On the more formal side, we conducted telephone interviews and solicited written survey answers to obtain detailed information from seventeen sets of identical and fraternal twins. These twins ranged in age from their mid-twenties to their early nineties. (We know how confusing twins can be, so we have included a "Twin Map" in Appendix I which provides demographic information on the most-quoted twins.)

You may be wondering where we found all of these twins to provide informal life stories for this book. Interestingly, we only know a few of them personally. The vast majority of the twins whom you will get to know as you move through the book came to us by coincidence, or by what we call "twincidence." Someone knew someone who knew someone who was a twin or who was related to a twin. Literally, through word-of-mouth, we were drawn to approach all of the twins who graciously gave of their time and energy to enrich our research. We will always be grateful to them for their gift to us—which we give to you in this book.

With the help of their stories and our own, we take you inside the twin relationship so you can understand it on a new level. Our goal was to unravel the mystery of twinship and reveal to nontwins what it *really* feels like to be a twin. Just like looking in a mirror (whether dancing or otherwise), as a twin you see aspects of yourself that you may or may not like. Not only is a twin a mirror from a strictly physical perspective, but also a twin provides a constant reflection of your own behavior.

Even though this image sometimes hits too close to home, we discovered that sharing the intimate dance of life with a twin presents a powerful opportunity for self-awareness and personal growth. And as we moved through our research, we found that the lessons we learned about twinship are not as far removed from all other relationships as we originally thought. In fact, many of our nontwin friends told us that our anecdotes about twins reminded them of experiences in their closest relationships.

All close relationships are filled with the need to communicate effectively, the desire to give and receive love, the sharing of life's pleasures and pains, and the hope of making time together the best that it can be. We now think that through this book any reader can gain, not only useful insights about twins, but also lessons that easily apply to anyone's search for successful, loving relationships of all types.

The process of writing this book has been a journey for us leading back to the basic joy found many years ago with that naked jig in front of the fridge. We hope to inspire this new dance in *your* life. We invite you to go ahead, strip away your inhibitions, peel back any doubts, let go of fears, open your eyes wide, and of course, throw off your clothes. Then you can begin your naked dance! (Refrigerators are not as conducive to viewing your dance these days, so you may need to resort to a mirror.) The key elements are joy and love as you watch yourself dance in front of your mirror and in your everyday life. Enjoy the giggles, and even the jiggles.

CHAPTER 1

A WOMB FOR TWO

✳

It's hard for me to describe the closeness I feel for my twin. She has been my closest possible friend and staunchest ally. Even when I didn't deserve her love, it was there for me. We are so close that we feel like mothers to each other's children. I don't think there are enough words to describe the closeness we share. It began before we were born.

—Jennifer, 44-year-old fraternal twin

Our closeness is a bond that no one would understand unless you are a twin. It is a closeness so tight, with so much unconditional caring and love for each other. I can't imagine going through life without my twin sister. That loss would truly be too much for me to bear.

—Joy, Jennifer's twin

All who would win joy must share it;
happiness was born a twin.

—Lord Byron

✸

"**M**rs. Sipes, you're going to have twins," Dr. Jackson told our mom a little too matter-of-factly. You can imagine her surprise at the sound of these words late in her sixth month of pregnancy. Visions of her two-year-old and four-year-old daughters waiting at home in that small house in Amarillo, Texas multiplied her weariness upon hearing this news.

Because of the enormous size of Mom's swollen belly, this routine pre-natal visit had started with an argument over the calculation of her due date. Mom sternly assured Dr. Jackson that she was well aware of the date of her conception and, therefore, the impending delivery date. To resolve the conflict, he ordered X-rays (a common practice in the late 1950s). Sure enough, she was right about her due date, but her "victory" was more than she had bargained for—as the X-ray film clearly revealed two tiny skeletons.

TWINS—WHAT ARE THE ODDS?

With our birth a few short months later, our parents and sisters unexpectedly became part of an elite club of families with twins—a club whose membership today is steadily increasing. Amazingly, one in eighty-one births in the United States results in a set of twins; of these, one-third are identical. The number of multiple births is on the rise due to scientific advances which can cause women to super-ovulate, thereby improving their odds of giving birth to more than one baby. Another contributing factor is that more women are deciding to have children later in life which increases the probability of multiple births. The chances of a twin touching your life are pretty good and are getting better all the time. Growing numbers of twins and other multiples signify a need to understand and appreciate how their lives are colored by the virtue of their shared existence.

There's no denying that the birth of twins carries with it a profound impact. Yet the greatest effect occurs for the two individuals who have come into this world together. Every stage of their lives is accompanied by the curiosity of others.

This has certainly been the case in our lives. We want to bring you into this world that you are so curious about, but also assist you in realizing that it's a very complex and unique place. Many torrents flow beneath the surface of the fantasy of life as twins.

WHAT ARE TWINS, ANYWAY?

The first step on our journey of many steps is to help you understand the definition of twins. It's impossible to talk in depth about twins without delving a little into the science that surrounds their creation. So that you have a foundation for the rest of this book, we need to take a moment here and become a bit academic.

Identical or Fraternal

Do you know the difference between identical and fraternal twins? There's a prevailing misconception that the definition of identical twins is merely that the twins look alike. While it's true that identical twins look like each other, the reason they're called identical is much deeper.

The creation of identical twins is truly a mystery. For some unknown reason, a fertilized egg basically loses its mind during its inner division and decides to split in two. The reasons for this decision still elude the greatest scientific minds. The result of the split is two humans who are genetically the same. Identical twins cannot be predicted or induced through any method of man-made fertilization. They are simply divinely inspired. Whether they look exactly alike or not (especially later in their lives), they are identical twins forever.

Another interesting aspect of identical twinning involves the fact that identical twins can only form at three different points, between days 5 and 9 after fertilization of the egg. Scientists don't know the consequences of the timing of the split, only that during a pregnancy three stages exist that will permit the formation of identical twins. If the split doesn't occur within that window of opportunity, identical twins aren't possible.

For fraternal twins, you could say that the timing was just perfect. Two sperm fertilize two eggs creating two babies simultaneously. Although fraternal twins are unusual, they are somewhat more predictable due to a genetic propensity for their development. If you have fraternal twins in your family, you're likely to see more fraternal twins blossom on the family tree. Fraternal twins often exhibit opposite traits, including being of the opposite sex. (Always remember that it is impossible for identical twins to be of the opposite sex, so be sure never to ask the parents of a set of boy-girl twins if they are identical!)

Independent of being identical or fraternal, the entire process of twinning is extremely fragile. The fact that, in about 55 percent of all twin conceptions, one twin dies before birth strongly suggests how complicated twinning truly is. Many times the parents didn't even know that the surviving baby had been a twin.

The delicate balance in nature that brings twins into being is wondrous indeed. Besides the miracle of twins' creation, they're also affected by sharing their mother's uterus. The long-lasting influence of that shared uterine development has been shown to have a substantial impact on twins.

IS IT IN THE GENES?

The now-famous 1979 Minnesota twin study conducted by Dr. Thomas Bouchard, Jr., addressed the issue of nature versus nurture in twins. He studied over one hundred sets of twins and triplets who were separated at birth. His hypothesis was that any shared traits which appeared between the separated twins would be genetic, since their environmental influences had been different. This theory did not completely hold true.

The amazing findings from these studies indicate that similar traits found in the twins did not seem to be grounded in genetics. For example, one set of identical male twins who were raised in different countries had personality quirks in common, such as storing rubberbands on their wrists, reading magazines back to front, and flushing the toilet before using it. Is this coincidence or genetics? Who knows? But it's important to note that such uncommon personality traits are not usually considered to be genetically encoded.

The Minnesota twin study supplies compelling evidence for the expansion of our definition of hereditary traits. In observing twins, it's obvious that genetics play a role that should not be underestimated. However, there is no way to factor in any influence that shared time *in utero* and infancy may provide.

Some Effects of Having a Wombmate

The numerous studies of twins reared apart seem to demonstrate that these pairs, when re-united, have astounding similarities. This fact is remarkable since the two usually have had such varying backgrounds. However, keep in mind that separated twins are treated like singletons in the worlds where they grow up. Therefore, they *never really* experience being looked at and treated as twins.

For instance, they do not undergo the constant comparison that twins who are raised together face. Their twin is not right by their side as a built-in behavioral mirror. Being raised apart allows each twin to develop his or her full genetic characteristics without the environmental pressure of being measured against the behavior/performance of the other. Therefore, whatever natural tendencies are inherent in each of the separated twins (including what they learned *in utero* or during any shared infancy) can be readily expressed without the added influence of being compared to one another. (This common comparison can sound something like this: "She's the tomboy; her sister is the feminine one" or "But your twin enjoys reading, why don't you?") Twins reared apart do not experience this side of twin life.

Ah, but twins raised together are under a different kind of pressure that drives their development into opposites. Though these twins will also exhibit similarities, they will most often show different personalities. Twins who are reared together are treated like—well, TWINS! They are constantly together, are dressed alike, are looked at as a combined entity, and are judged against each other. Under these circumstances, is it any wonder that each twin strives for a way to be seen as an individual?

Each twin will begin to take on a personality trait that he or she can call his or her own. Then the twin will express his or her "individual" trait, for the most part, exclusively. Their twin will, in turn, exhibit an equally "individual" opposite trait. The end result is a paradox of two people who look alike, but who are really *very* different from one another. So much for the myth that twins are exactly the same. The truth is that most twins develop their own personal contrasts to gain an identity apart from the twinship—a job that twins raised away from one another do not have to tackle. (We discuss all of this in more detail in later chapters.)

All kinds of forces, some from surprising sources,

play a role in the life of twins. Situations inside and outside of the twinship blend together to construct a fascinating world for twins. A world that is difficult to imagine, unless you are a twin. But, unexpectedly, it's a world that really is very similar to the sphere that exists around all close relationships. Our desire is to open up this new world for you. Welcome inside!

CHAPTER 2

THE TWIN BOND

✳

The bond we have is difficult to describe in words and in some ways it can only be truly known by someone else who is a twin. There's an unspoken closeness which transcends time, distance, and amount of physical contact. My twin is an extension of myself.

—Walt, 39-year-old identical twin

As we've gotten older, we've spent less time physically together but we realize more and more how much we mean to one another. We are now at a point in our relationship that we don't need to say anything to know how we feel about one another. There's a connection that cannot truly be explained and will never change.

—John, Walt's twin

Twins often find themselves to be the most fascinating plaything of all.

—Clegg

"What's it really like to be twins?" We've been asked this question hundreds of times over the years. Though we can't even begin to conceive of experiencing life as a "singleton," we think the best way to answer this question is to bring you in touch with the twin bond. All twins share a bond that is, to say the least, miraculous. Given the nature of their lives, it's not at all surprising that twins inherently have this bond. From conception, powerful internal forces play on twins which act to fuse the pair into an extraordinary unit.

Twins share a very intimate beginning due to the close quarters assigned to them *in utero*. Nothing generates more bonding than having your own "wombmate." Our mom insists that from her perspective, we most certainly had our first fisticuffs in those cramped quarters. We know, however, that more importantly, we shared our first hugs there, too.

INSIDE THE TWIN BOND

In this time when "bonding" seems to be the order of the day—there's male bonding, female bonding, mother-to-child bonding—we submit twin bonding. The unusual thing about the twin bond, however, is that we don't have to work on it; it's innate and essentially cannot be denied.

Even if you are a twin, this bond can be difficult to understand and even more troublesome to articulate. Problems have arisen all of our lives with family, friends, and significant others who are not able to fully grasp the character of this bond. A better understanding of the twin bond should aid twins and nontwins alike to accept and to work with the bond more effectively.

Defining the twin bond is a task of epic proportions. Asking twins themselves, both identical and fraternal, to put the magic of the bond into words, we were told:

"It's more special than a best friend."

"There aren't enough words to describe the bond we have as twins."

"There can be no one closer to me than my twin. Sometimes friends, as well as spouses, have had a hard time truly understanding the bond and closeness we have."

"It's like a soulmate: we're connected at the heart for life."

These esoteric thoughts somehow make sense to

other twins, but aren't very helpful in clarifying the twin bond for nontwins. Therefore, we think, the spirit of the bond can best be explained by taking a closer look at the uniqueness of twins' lives. Growing up at the same time lends itself to a lifetime of sharing and companionship, forging a bond that is deep and self-sustaining.

Me and My Shadow

We shared a double bed throughout childhood and into adolescence. In our big childhood bed, our twin bond was nurtured. Our mom remembers coming in to kiss us goodnight when we were children. She says with a smile, "You two would be lying face-to-face, sound asleep, gently holding each other's hands. It was *impossible*, at that moment, to tell you apart."

This bond is further exemplified through heartfelt remarks made by identical twins Chris and Cathy, on separate occasions. Chris revealed her deepest feelings for Cathy when she declared, "She's the only person I can truly say I would lay down my life for—that her well-being is more important than mine." While Cathy confessed, "I think the one thing I worry about the most is that my twin will die. I can't imagine going on myself without her." This everlasting commitment is a result of the security twins find in each other's company—based largely on the strong foundation built from so much time spent together.

Interestingly, all this time together, coupled with *literal* simultaneous development, can result in the bond being even stronger than other sibling-to-sibling bonds. Just imagine learning to touch, laugh, crawl, walk, talk, potty train, tie your shoes, read, write, dance, survive puberty, discover the opposite sex, and experience virtually all other growing pains and gains with someone else exactly your age! Imagine your very own built-in best friend. Imagine never being alone.

With this in mind, you can see that twins, for the most part, never have the feeling of being absolutely alone. Your twin is basically your shadow—where you go, so goes your twin. Especially as small children, twins rarely experience complete solitude. This continual contact creates an invisible alliance that attaches the twins to each other.

Constant Companion

Shared time is a constant in the lives of twins. You can't help but develop a close bond with someone who is growing up at the same time you are and from whom you are seldom (if ever) separated. In fact, most twins reported that they were almost teenagers before they ever spent the night apart from one another.

The twin bond means having a perpetual companion who just happens to be perfectly compatible. It's like taking the very best day you've ever had with a loved one—a day when you were really in sync: you wanted exactly the same thing to eat, preferred to do the same activity, communicated without speaking, couldn't wipe the smiles off your faces, laughed endlessly, and enjoyed each other's company completely.

Now take that sensation and stretch it over a lifetime. *That* almost describes what it's like to have a twin. Although you may have experienced this type of day a few times in your life with a friend, family member, or spouse, this "best day" scenario is more often than not routine in the life of twins.

As a result of this feeling, twins often want their twin to be part of life's most special moments. Suzanne confided in us that she didn't want her friends or parents to attend an important singing audition with her. She only wanted her twin brother to be there: "I knew that just his presence there would have a calming effect on me." Suzanne was right. She sang before the judges (and her twin brother) and got the job.

Suzanne's story shows how the twin bond can serve as a conduit for information or feelings to pass between twins. Unspoken support is a given between twins. Therefore, throughout their lives, when twins are apart they have a heightened awareness of their twin's absence. They can feel a void or emptiness merely because their twin missed the moment. Yet, paradoxically, even when separated, there also exists an underlying feeling of one's twin being present. These are two sides of the same coin. Both reactions are a response to the enduring effects of the twin bond.

Undeniable Devotion

The bond is magical and mysterious. It's the cement that holds twins together, and ironically, the wedge that can come between them and other people. Being very intense and often uncontrollable, this bond can create misunderstandings by seeming to have a life all its own. It can leave the impression that twins don't need anyone else but each other.

We became aware of the impact of our bond on others during our teenage years when it was obvious that our first boyfriends were not exactly thrilled with our bond. They felt that *they* ought to be the center of our universes—and told us so. We spent most of our teenage years trying to balance our bond, while striving to create bonds with others. This task is difficult for twins because they already have a built-in soulmate. The forces that drive nontwins to make friends are not as dominant for twins.

Cindy, an identical twin, spelled out just how the

bond can produce tension in other relationships: "When I was married, my husband was very jealous of my twin. He once told me, 'You would probably be more upset if your sister died than if I did.' Unthinkingly, I responded, 'Yes.' This comment caused a huge argument that lasted for days."

Cindy found it impossible to help her husband understand the closeness she shared with her twin sister. A struggle for priority in Cindy's life was a draining force on the marriage. Eventually, that marriage ended. Cindy shook her head and surmised, "Spouses need to recognize the sacred territory of the twin relationship. To have a relationship with a twin, the non-twin needs to accept the 'twin thing' [you know, the twin bond]—not be jealous of it. Life is so much easier when they work *with* the twin relationship, not *against* it."

This larger-than-life bond can be frustrating to others because it's so meaningful for twins. We agree with Cindy's advice to try recognition and acceptance of the twin bond. Also, remember that twins' passion for their twinship is not intended to minimize anyone else's importance in their lives. On the contrary, we believe that the twin bond intensifies the ability to give and receive love.

Being a twin is a gift that, at its deeper levels, can only truly be shared with your twin. After that, for us, the love we have for others in our lives is just as rich, only on a different playing field.

(Tips for helping nontwins accept the twin bond appear in Appendix II.)

WHAT'S MINE IS OURS:
A LIFE OF SHARING

The twin bond is further strengthened by virtue of a lifetime of sharing. From the nutrients supplied through the mother's amniotic fluid to the small space inside the womb, the life of sharing for twins begins at conception. Ask any set of twins what they shared growing up and the overwhelming response will be, "EVERYTHING!" Sharing is definitely a buzz word for twin life.

It's Only Natural

It has been described by one twin as, "Our sharing was a natural thing. We never wanted it to be any other way." The lifestyle of sharing seems to have a positive influence on twins. It helps to cultivate a willingness to share outside of the twinship as well.

Being a twin really plays a part in preventing self-ishness from taking root. Perpetual sharing contributes to twins having a generous nature. Identical twin Walt believes a life of sharing positively affected his and his twin brother's personalities as adults. "We are both very giving people," Walt declared. "I think this stems from always having shared as a twin and this was the norm in our lives." His twin brother John put it this way, "In terms of our thoughts, our morals, our beliefs, we share all of these and we spend time sharing our perceptions on these things, too."

Sharing just naturally goes with being twins. We know that we find much joy in continually sharing this world with one another. It's unspoken, but we just know, that whatever we have, we share. In fact, we even shared our first date.

Our Daddy started a tradition with our older sisters that for the twelfth birthday celebration, he would take the birthday girl out on her first "date." His rationale was that the next year would bring on the teen-age years and his special place would be lost forever in the maze and haze of boy-craze.

We watched patiently as our older sisters Terri, then Brenda, got all dressed up to go out with Daddy to any place of their choosing. Finally our much-anticipated twelfth birthday came. With great enthusiasm we shared our date with Daddy. It never occurred to us, or to Daddy for that matter, that we could go separately. So, off we went to a delightful dinner at our favorite fancy restaurant for a steak (which we shared) and then to a rodeo.

This event also started our ritual of sharing meals in restaurants—much to the frustration of others. To this day, we still split entrees when we go out to eat. Nancy's husband Stu put it quite pointedly when he asked her about this habit: "Why do you always insist on cutting the food in half with me? When you and Janna share things, you never cut it in half!" You see with each other, we just *know* when we've eaten our half—no tangible division is necessary.

Carpooling

During adolescence for twins, perhaps the most commonly shared item is a car. Identical twins Earl and Gearl told us about the shared car of their teen years. These delightful, over-60-year-old twins grew up in rural west Texas. Having a dependable car was a necessity for proper socializing. But for Earl and Gearl, this one-car situation turned out to be problematic for their dating purposes. As Earl noted, "We had to take turns going out on dates. That didn't set well with the one who couldn't go." The solution was easy for these very close twins. They began a tradition of double-dating! This remedy was doubly rewarding for them; they got to go out on a date, and they also got to be together.

Some twins share the driving assignment of the car in their joint custody, while others have a designated driver. In our case, the driving responsibility was left up to Nancy. She was the appointed driver and Janna was the keeper of the keys, as well as the self-appointed navigator.

[Nancy: *Why I was given this dubious honor, I don't know. It certainly wasn't due to my prowess behind the wheel. Our shared navy-blue 1968 Ford Galaxy 500 had the dings and scrapes to testify to my unrefined driving skills. Except for the sheer terror that came from just riding with me, surprisingly we never encountered any problems with sharing a car. In fact, I didn't even mind "Driving Miss Janna!"*]

The Twin Trust Bank

Not only did we share the obvious things such as a bedroom (and bed), clothes (most twins tout a double wardrobe), toys, books, friends, food, and eventually a car, we also shared our deepest, darkest thoughts and dreams with each other from a very early age. This phenomenon is common for twins.

We simply could not (and cannot to this day) keep a secret from each other. Always knowing that our confidences were safe within the twinship, we shared them freely. Our sister Terri laughs when she says, "I know I only have to tell one of you any of the family news. The other one will torture you with brain waves until you spill the details to her also."

Sharing secrets with your twin is instinctive due to the immense trust that exists within the twinship. A lifetime of this type of giving and receiving builds up a positive balance in what we call the " twin trust bank."

Our trust bank was, to say the least, overflowing. When we were children, once we got settled into our spots at bedtime—we each had our own side of the bed—we would entrust our treasured secrets and fanciful dreams to one another. Those innocent conversations would often turn into gales of laughter, causing a knock on the wall from our parents' adjoining room with a warning to go to sleep. This command usually resulted in our laughing even harder, forcing us to dig ourselves deeper under the covers in an attempt to muffle our giggles. For twins, every night is a veritable slumber party!

Our mom reminded us that our uncontrollable tendency to spend nights chatting instead of sleeping caused our parents to make a trial run at putting us in separate bedrooms. When we were ten years old, Nancy moved into our sister Terri's room, while our other sister Brenda came to bunk with Janna in the former "twins" bedroom.

This experiment failed miserably. Our parents finally gave up when they discovered us in the same bed more mornings than not. You see, after bedtime, we would merely talk Terri into sleeping with Brenda in the room that was next to our parents' bedroom. That way, Mom and Dad couldn't hear us, we could resume our secret conversations, and our trust bank confidences grew and grew.

Since twinship is such a safe place for confidence swapping, those shared little childhood secrets ripen into prized pubescent hopes and ultimately serious adult dreams. Sharon, a fraternal twin, explained this tendency: "There are certain things that I don't confide in anyone else because I don't trust them like I do my twin."

Too Close for Comfort?

Although twin trust is easy to maintain between twins, the security of years of mutual deposits and withdrawals from the trust bank doesn't transpose easily onto the world that exists outside of the twinship. Often, we've ended up sharing too much of ourselves too easily, too soon. Trouble holding back in new relationships is a by-product of the twin trust bank. Twins have a tendency to seek in others the closeness they have with their twins because their twinship is their gold standard for love.

Additionally, twins' seemingly unbridled tolerance for closeness in relationships isn't always well-received in the nontwin world. At times friends and acquaintances can find twins' acceptance for closeness to be an overwhelming, uncomfortable experience, especially early on. One of Janna's friends once asked, "Do you want to spend this much time with *all* of your friends? Sometimes this just seems like too much togetherness for me." You see, growing up, twins get a distorted view of relationships because they usually don't have a great need for space or time alone. As Renee, an identical twin, so aptly put it, "Being together is our plan for life."

The bottom line is that the specialness of the twin bond can't be completely reproduced in nontwin relationships. Twins can achieve intimate closeness in other relationships, but it is essential to remember that others cannot substitute for their twin.

We found that we need to be careful not to give too much of ourselves to others too early in relationships. In our nontwin relationships, we both had to learn to hold a little back and keep some secrets to ourselves that could have been easily and faithfully shared with each other.

(Tips for twins on balancing a high tolerance for closeness with the need for space are also in Appendix II.)

Good Tools for Other Relationships

Learning how to express love, rely on each other, spend huge quantities of time together, and keep a secret are all part of the early lessons of twinship. These teachings transcend twinships, however, and provide a strong foundation for all other relationships. As Rhonda and Renee's mother reminded them often, "You are so lucky to be twins. I see you using communication, compromise, and collaboration everyday. These are such good tools for your twin relationship—and for your future marriages!" Twinship is a dress rehearsal for all relationships.

The twin bond is the link that lets twins know how special their relationship is. Although it's obvious that twins would fuel and nurture this bond, you might be surprised to know that practically everyone else, outside the twinship, provides their share of the glue that helps hold the twins together.

CHAPTER 3

EXTERNAL FORCES AT PLAY ON THE TWIN BOND

✳

It's so funny how people see us as one, even our parents treated us as a combined entity. Therefore, when my twin got good grades, we both were praised. Conversely, when one of us was bad, it was just assumed that we were both rotten.

—Chris, 41-year-old identical twin

Our family treated us as "one." This was especially true on our birthday. We had a joint celebration and our relatives would always give us the same gift without thinking of us as individuals. I guess that's just how the world sees twins.

—Cathy, Chris' twin

I was raised to sense what someone wanted me to be and to be that kind of person. It took me a long time not to judge myself through someone else's eyes.

—Sally Field

✳

Carol was laughing at herself when she told us this story:

"I really thought it was Nancy! I was walking into the Del Mar Fair and I thought I saw her walking next to me. I began frantically waving, wondering why in the world she wasn't responding. Finally, I asked, rather indignantly, 'Dr. Sipes, are you just going to ignore me?'

"To my amazement, the woman I'd addressed declared, 'You must have me confused with my sister, Nancy.' I remember doing a double take and declaring, 'Well, if you are her sister, you must be her twin because you look just like her!' She replied with a big grin, 'As a matter of fact, I am her twin sister, Janna.'"

Have you ever been mistaken for someone else like this? Or have you ever been called by the wrong name? These things happen to us all the time. We forget to mention the fact that we have a twin, until we run into acquaintances like Carol who remind us, not so subtly, that there's someone else out there who is wearing our face! These types of external forces play as important a role in twins' lives as the innate urge to bond with each other. Outside forces (including, not only family and friends, but also total strangers) help to foster twins' closeness and contribute to the blurring of twins' feelings of individuality.

The second most frequently asked question for us

is: "Are you and your twin exactly alike?" This question epitomizes many nontwins' view of twins—that we are like one person, exact duplicates of one another.

In lieu of screaming from the top of our lungs, "NO! We are not just alike! We are individuals," we decided to show you how other people's perceptions of twins sustain the twin bond. Not surprisingly, these outside influences can also trigger a desperate need in twins to express their own individuality.

Outside factors such as being dressed alike, receiving shared gifts, enduring strangers' reactions to twins, being called "twin" instead of your proper name, and submitting to constant comparisons are all part of life for twins. With everyone else's attention focused on twins as a twosome, it's easy to see why twins themselves gravitate toward their bond with each other, while simultaneously yearning to experience a separation from it.

This treatment produces a sense of over-identity with one's twin and an under-identity with one's self. Let's investigate how extrinsic forces operate on the twin bond and how being regarded as one and the same steers twins on a quest to be individuals.

Matching Outfits

Perhaps the single biggest external influence on the

twin bond is being dressed alike. It's hard to find words to describe this experience!

Have you ever gone to a party or shown up at work and discovered someone else wearing your outfit? Do you remember your reaction? You probably felt a little embarrassed and maybe even a tad bit offended. Did it seem like it took some of your specialness and uniqueness away?

Well, for most twins, being dressed the same as someone else is a way of life and, amazingly enough, actually creates the feeling of "twin-ness." Every day twins feel just the opposite of what nontwins feel when they see someone dressed like them. It's one of the great paradoxes of twins' lives. Instead of feeling bad about seeing someone dressed like you, it's your sense of identity.

The dilemma is magnified from parental attempts to nurture (and perhaps show off) the specialness of the twins, while at the same time facing the challenge of fostering individuality in the twins. Individuality often comes out the loser, as dressing alike reinforces the world's view that twins are like one person.

Treated as One

In a strange way, dressing twins in the same clothes is symbolic of the manner in which twins are often treated. As two darling children are paraded through grocery stores, shopping malls, and family gatherings to represent human clones, the message to the world is that these two humans *are* exactly alike. The world responds accordingly. It's merely a function of deductive reasoning: they look alike, they dress alike, therefore, they are alike.

For us, this message gained momentum as we got older. By the time we were about eight years old and given the choice to dress alike or not, we still dressed alike. We couldn't let go of our conditioned need to meet the outside world as a combined entity. Our union was signaled by our matching attire.

When Do You Stop Dressing Alike?
(Maybe Never!)

We dressed alike until we were in junior high school, when our mom had to insist that we start exploring other options. It was funny; we had to wean ourselves off dressing alike. First, we had the same outfit in different colors. Once the spell was broken, we began to see some identity as individuals in the different colors. Finally, by high school our transition led us to completely individual clothes and the best dividend of all, two wardrobes!

Most twins become very attached to dressing alike.

Even fraternal twins are not immune to this dressing alike bug. Fraternal twin Karen found it to be a wonderful part of her twinship. "Oh, yes, we dressed alike from infancy through grade school. Even when we were teenagers, we would often dress alike just for the fun of it," she explained.

Vivian, a 91-year-old fraternal twin, agreed, "We were raised with a very Victorian view. Mother and Father felt twins must always look alike and dress alike. My sister and I dressed alike through our college years." Vivian's statement emphasizes how the external view of what twins are "supposed to be" plays such an enormous part in their lives. Again, the recurring theme—twins are seen as one entity and are frequently treated that way.

Some twins continue to dress alike throughout their lives. Esther and Besse are over-80-year-old identical twins who still wear matching (or identical) clothes simply because they "enjoy the experience." Quite often twins have similar tastes and end up dressing alike almost by accident. We are frequently astounded to meet each other and find we are wearing practically the same outfit. In fact, recently we met up toting the exact same purse. Nancy bought hers while shopping with her husband. Janna picked hers up during a shopping spree in Arizona with our sister, Brenda. We had to be careful when grabbing our purses so as not to walk off with the wrong one!

Whether identical or fraternal, twins grow up accepting the idea of dressing alike. Many find the habit to be enjoyable and fun. However, those twins who are forced to keep up the practice once they have tired of it may harbor some resentment. The decision to wear identical clothes is a personal matter between twins. When the time comes to participate in their own clothing selections, the fairest approach is to involve the twins themselves in the ultimate choice.

THE SAME GIFT

Birthday celebrations are exciting experiences for children, likely to include a party complete with birthday cake, hats, games, friends, and, of course, birthday presents. A birthday for twins is a day of monumental sharing. Here's a peek at a typical twin celebration.

There's only one party for the two individuals. When it comes time for the cake, the twins' mother brings out one cake with one set of candles. After she lights the candles, both twins lean forward to blow them out. In our case, Mom would then say, "Hurry, girls, and open your presents together."

We knew we had to open the same present at the same time because we received the same gift. If one of us was faster on the draw, the other would have the surprise spoiled. (This scene was replayed at Christmas.) The party was always great fun, but it was a shared experience. We don't know how it feels to have a birthday party all to yourself where you are the center of attention. In twins' lives, "the twins" are the center of attention.

The intentional duplication of gifts is a sincere attempt to show no favoritism, or at least to minimize the potential that favoritism would ever be construed. That one twin might consider his or her twin's present to be the better one is probably too much for parents of twins to bear!

Twins accept the "same-gift phenomenon" as a fact of life. Identical twin John resigned himself to this event: "It was no big deal, really. We knew we would always get the same gift, but it was still fun to get a present anyway. He had his and I had mine." John's perspective shows how twins have a way of acknowledging an identical gift as personal to themselves and of telling even the most exact gifts apart.

As children, we collected stuffed animals. In fact, one entire wall of our bedroom was covered with a giant pegboard which proudly displayed all of our identical pairs of stuffed animals. They hung adorably by the colorful, satin ribbons around their necks. Our collection was always increased on gift-giving occasions as we would often receive the exact same stuffed animal from some family member. It was amazing to our family that, from the moment we opened our gifts, we could instantly find a distinguishing characteristic in those two identical dogs so that we knew which one belonged to whom. We never mixed them up.

The symbolism of this exercise was lost on us as children. Now, in retrospect, we seemed to be telling the world that, no matter how much alike things appear, uniqueness is there to be seen.

YOUR CONTRIBUTION TO THE TWIN BOND

If you think twins overindulge in the twin bond, remember, we are not alone! Though their attachment to each other is genetically encoded from conception, this devotion is further strengthened by external influences such as yourself.

What?! You didn't realize you have an effect on the perpetuation of the twin bond? Well, you do! Here's how.

Strangers' Reactions to Twins: A Loss of Privacy?

Picture the scene: You see someone pushing a baby stroller big enough to hold more than one child. You think, oh, they have two children. But you quickly (albeit almost unconsciously!) do a double take to see if those two children are twins. Once you see that they're the same, or about the same size, you sprint tiptoedly over to the parent to begin the "ogle and quiz routine," saying things like, "They are soooo cute! Are they twins?" "How far apart are they?" "Are they identical?" "Which one is older?" "What are their names?"

Go ahead, admit it. You've done it, haven't you? We have to confess that *even we* have done it. The temptation is simply too strong to resist. All babies are pretty irresistible, but two (or more!) at the same time overwhelm our inhibitions and jostle our curiosity.

This reaction happens every day in the lives of twins. Parents of twins tell us that they *never* leave home with their twins without getting bombarded with questions about them. Our mom confided in us, "We lost our family privacy once you were born. It was incredible how people felt comfortable asking even the most personal questions about twins." Surprisingly, women even asked her detailed questions about her pregnancy and delivery.

To save you the trouble of asking, we share our mom's story with you to vividly illustrate how external forces play a part in the lives of twins—even before they are born.

Mom gave birth to us in 1957 when they still anesthetized mothers to minimize the pain of childbirth. Therefore, she wasn't awake when we emerged one after the other, a scant four minutes apart.

Although unconscious during our birth, she did remember that she woke up before we were born to deafening silence and blinding lights on the operating table. Through squinted eyes she could barely make out a blurred background of large panes of glass and two masked faces in front of her. One face seemed to shout from a tunnel far, far away, "Mrs. Sipes, Mrs. Sipes, can you hear us? You are in the operating room theater. You do remember giving your permission for other doctors to observe your multiple birth delivery, don't you?" Unable to speak, she numbly remembered that, yes, she had given her permission. What Mom didn't realize at that time was that by merely having twins, she had also unknowingly given her permission for all the world to be a part of her experience and our lives.

Still a Side-Show Attraction

As twins grow up, they don't consciously think about the fact that they are twins, but other people's reactions serve as a constant reminder and help to reinforce the twin bond. It seems curiosity doesn't wane even when twins are beyond the baby carriage stage. As identical twin Rhonda, a young college student confirmed, "When we are with each other, I often forget we are twins until people start staring and pointing." With this perception that twins are some type of attraction, you can see why twins sense themselves to be on display as one unit.

We are not saying that approaching twins with excitement and interest is taboo. Quite the opposite is true. We love talking about experiencing life as twins (as did most of the twins we researched). What we want to do is raise your awareness of how you react to twins.

We enjoy honest, direct enthusiasm about our twinship. Recently, we were at the airport lugging two bags each and rushing to catch a flight. As we struggled through the automatic door, a man passed by, turned his head slightly, and with a huge grin asked, "Are you twins?" It made us both smile and respond, "Yes," in stereo. He merely replied, "That's cool!" and kept walking. Now that's a great way to approach twins—interested, but not intrusive.

Remember that twins, even as children, recognize that they are the center of attention because there are two of them. Whether they gain comfort with the attention or not, twins realize that they are novel—as a twosome!

This continuous reinforcement of the "two-ness" of twins definitely nourishes the twin bond, but as discussed later, a true sense of individual identity starts to starve.

Is My Name Twin?

People who know twins have a clear impact on the twin bond. One major contribution made by well-meaning nontwins is the use of the word "twin" as a name. We were probably seven years old before we realized that "twin" was not part of our names!

Logically, it makes sense why someone would use "twin" instead of a name. Let's face it, identical twins are darned hard to tell apart and fraternal twins, even if they do not look that much alike, force you to remember two names instead of one. (Now is Jay the one with red hair and freckles or is that Ray?)

Even though we can rationalize why someone would use "twin" as a name, you can see that this simple act can help bond twins together and cloud any sense of distinction they may have about themselves. Consider how you'd feel if you were called "boy" or "girl" all your life, instead of being called by your given name. Would you start to think of yourself as a nonentity and not see yourself as an individual who gets called by a name that's unique to you? (Unless you and your brothers are all named Darrell, but then that's another story . . .)

Our favorite Aunt Betty put a little "twist" to this idea by calling us the "Twisters." She would laugh in her deep-throated contagious way and say, "Well, you two are twins, but you are also sisters. That makes you the Twisters!" It did not help us gain an understanding of our individuality, but it was fun to be called something unique.

Our research suggests that twins are somewhat split on their feelings about being called "twin." Here are a few of their responses:

"It made me proud and happy to be called twin. It was fun." But her twin disagreed: *"I didn't really like being called twin or 'the twins.' I felt it showed they didn't see us as having separate names or being individuals. It was as if we always came as a package."*
—*Rhonda and Renee, 30-year-old identicals*

"I don't like being called twin. We do have names."
—*Linda, 15-year-old fraternal twin*

"Being called twin did not bother me a bit. I took it as a compliment indicating a unique feeling that my twin brother and I were something special."
—*Gearl, 64-year-old identical twin*

"Our dad still calls us twin to this day and we are over forty! I don't really mind because I believe our feeling of individuality comes from within."
—*Cindy, 42-year-old identical twin*

These thoughts show that as special as it is to be a twin, it's also important to be thought of as an individual. Walt told us that he doesn't remember being called "twin" so much but that he and John were often called by their last name by people in school. "This was because they didn't know which twin they were addressing," he said, "and because they lumped us together as the same." Mixed emotions resulted from this external force. Walt felt bothered at not being treated as an individual, yet felt good about being a twin. This is a fine line to walk. Stated simply, twins want to enjoy the blessing of the twinship, while being given some recognition as individuals.

We're sure that all of this is very confusing! Even in our family, our step-brother was frustrated when we told him that being called "twin" was depersonalizing to us. He threw up his hands and exclaimed, "Man, I thought it was a way to show you how special I think your relationship is. You two are the only people in my life I can call 'twin.' I thought I *was* treating you as unique." His attitude speaks to the dichotomy of this situation—being twins makes us distinctive, but being called "twin" makes us feel like we are not distinct. Get it?

MISSION IMPOSSIBLE:
TRY TO TELL US APART, BUT *PLEASE*. . .

. . . DON'T COMPARE US

One of the challenges in knowing twins is learning to tell them apart. Both identical and fraternal twins report that they are often mixed up by family and friends. One natural tendency for nontwins is to resort to comparisons of the twins in order to try to grasp some behavior, mannerism, or trait that distinguishes one twin from the other.

What's the Difference?

Identical twins recognize that they are hard to tell apart (in spite of *not* being able to see how much they look alike). Gearl affirmed, "We don't see it, but they say we have the same smile and voice. In school only Mother and Dad could tell us apart—by the way we walked."

The challenge of telling identical twins apart often brought comical moments to our family. When we were infants, our mom left us with her father while she ran an errand that was to take an hour or so. Granddad felt confident in his ability to manage two sleeping babies. In fact, he was a little too confident.

Mom attempted to instruct him on how to feed us if we awoke. She recalled that he rolled his eyes and grunted, "I've raised six kids of my own; you don't have to tell me how to handle this."

As you can guess, we did wake up—both at the same time, screaming loudly. It must have been quite a scene for as Granddad recounted it, he would pick one of us up for feeding and calming, but the other one would get so loud that he would switch babies. After this went on for a few minutes, he lost track of who had eaten and who had not. Mom arrived to find all three of us near hysteria. One of us had over-eaten and the other was over-hungry. Granddad was over-exhausted. Bless his heart, he never did learn to tell us apart, nor did he ever agree to baby-sit alone again!

But, granddads take heart, even moms can mix up their twins. Rhonda told this bath-time story: "My mom explained how she gave one of us a bath when we were really little and then she tried to give the other one a bath. But that one screamed and screamed. She finally realized that she tried to give the same baby a bath twice."

You really can learn to tell twins apart. There is *always* a distinguishing characteristic that you can use to differentiate even identical twins. Ours is easy; Janna has a cowlick in her bangs and Nancy does not. Of course, it is your job to remember which one has *the* characteristic.

(Just a reminder: Some tidbits appear in Appendix II to help nontwins find a way out of this twin-maze!)

Ironically, the one way to tell twins apart is by looking for a difference between them. Such dissimilar characteristics can be a godsend in keeping twins straight. However, as desirable as it is to find a distinguishing trait, it is equally important never to assume that the other twin does not have that same characteristic.

Comparisons of twins sound something like this: "X is the quiet twin, Y is the loud twin." "X is the actor, Y is the scholar." "X is the funny twin, Y is the serious twin," and so on.

As we go through our lives, comparisons are standard treatment for everyone. Nontwins are frequently measured against other siblings, their friends, or even their parents when they were that age. You've probably experienced the frustration of being held up to a standard created by someone else.

For twins, it's simply an exaggerated version of that reality. Being a twin provides a built-in comparative study model. No matter what you do when you're a twin, there's always someone standing right next to you (both literally and figuratively) either doing the same thing (better or worse) or not doing the same thing as you. Either way, twins get compared to each other.

One identical twin, Renee, shared angry feelings about this situation. "We always absolutely hated being compared to each other. It caused us to be so competitive. Those people who are so insensitive as to compare who is 'better' or 'prettier' are not worth listening to." She and her twin sister are athletes. They felt that playing sports was competitive enough without others reducing the judgment of their performance down to just the two of them. In our lives, once one of us was dubbed into a category (Nancy's the outgoing twin, Janna's the shy twin), we were pigeon-holed there for years. Not only did other people view us that way (probably in an attempt to tell us apart), but also we saw ourselves in those roles without even thinking about it. It was as though we accepted the roles we were cast in by the outside world's attempts to tell us apart.

I'M UNIQUE, BUT ONLY TO MY TWIN

Given all this outside stimulation, the twin bond flourishes. Twins get comfortable with the twinship and being seen as one entity. They usually accept being a twin as a role in life.

However, the other role a twin has is the person he or she is when with his or her twin. Think about it. A twin would describe it like this:

"The only person who does *not* treat me like a twin is my twin. My twin treats me like an individual, never thinking about the fact that I am her twin. To my twin, I am a singleton! I am a playmate, a friend, a confidante, a rival, a side-kick, a constant companion—but never a twin. My twin is the only person who does not at some time or another react to me as a twin. No calling me 'twin'; no confusing me with herself; no staring and pointing; I am just me."

Inside the twin relationship, individuals evolve. The outside pressure of whatever pigeon-hole the world has put you in no longer applies. Twins are the "people they really are" within their twinship. Finding the balance for those "real" people in the outside world is a challenge for most twins. (This issue is discussed in Chapter 7, "The Yin and Yang of Twinship.")

For our purposes here, it's important to note that since a twin's twin is the only person who can truly see a twin as an individual, the relationship that develops between the two of them is something very close and extremely special. External influences drive the twins toward each other, both because they are viewed as one entity outside the twinship, and because the twins can find themselves as individuals inside the twin bond.

All forces seem to work to push twins together as one. However, inside, twins are no different from you. Each one wants to know who he or she is as a person. A twin's search is more complicated by virtue of having a built-in mirror—someone who reflects his or her life. As a result, many things are happening inside the twin bond. Two people are experiencing the closest relationship possible. One of our friends described it perfectly, "A twinship is the only true, emotionally intimate relationship that is designed to be platonic." You can't get much closer than that.

While living inside a twinship, twins learn all kinds of ways to make the relationship more comfortable. They tailor many of life's day-to-day activities to fit their situation. For instance, their unique communication style evolves into its own language—what we call "twinspeak."

CHAPTER 4

TWINSPEAK IS A FOREIGN LANGUAGE

✳

My twin and I have actually spoken for each other and we often have the same thoughts. I think this is because we have shared a lifetime of experiences and the similarity for what each other is thinking is there. . . . At times when there's a third party involved, my twin and I can simply look at each other and know what the other is thinking without even using words.

—Karen, 36-year-old fraternal twin

Karen and I can get lost in our own little world. We can be alone together even in a crowd. In that world, we share all our experiences and confide in each other.

—Sharon, Karen's twin

It is a luxury to be understood.

—Ralph Waldo Emerson

✳

Our Uncle Larry loves to tell the story that epitomizes our special twinspeak. Larry is our mother's youngest brother who was only 13 years old when we were born. In those days, he was one of our most frequent and favorite visitors.

Typically, when Uncle Larry arrived, we'd burst into a giggling frenzy, knowing that he'd always pick both of us up at the same time. (It seemed to be a family delight to get to hold a baby in each arm.) On this certain occasion, we were about nine months old, sitting on the floor of the kitchen in our small home in Amarillo, Texas.

Larry noticed to his dismay that his entrance had not created the expected enthusiastic reaction from us. He remembered our faces being furrowed in frowns with angry grunts and gestures emitting from both of us. Looking back, Larry shakes his head and laughs, "You two were in your own world. It was obvious to me that you were arguing about something that you both understood all too clearly, even though the rest of us were clueless."

This presumed-serious argument lasted several minutes. "Then suddenly," Larry recalls, "just like magic, the whole incident was over and you both began smiling and playing merrily with each other." Our own way of communicating resolved whatever problem had existed.

TWINSPEAK DEFINED

From talking in unison to perceiving each other's feelings, twins develop and demonstrate well-established strategies for relating to one another which are not necessarily practical for use with anyone else. If you know twins, you've probably observed their unique patterns of communication. If you don't know twins, you can guess that they must have some special way of communicating. Nontwins often think twins are in a separate world—particularly after witnessing their nonverbal exchanges. This is twinspeak.

The twin bond and its communication characteristics are lifelong and self-perpetuating. Twins communicate in a way that's different from the rest of the world. However, twinspeak, while effective in the twinship, doesn't usually translate into a recognizable language for others. If you have a relationship with a twin, you've probably been frustrated by twinspeak. We hope this chapter will help you gain some understanding of how to deal with it.

Baby Twinspeak

The origin of twinspeak is similar to the beginning of the "language" that most infants and toddlers invent to communicate their feelings to siblings and parents.

Such childhood secret language is known as *cryptoglossia*. Certainly, it is seen in young siblings who have eager older siblings to translate their utterances for the world around them. In addition, many parents are able to understand their children's apparent jibberish, to the amazement of onlookers.

Twins also readily engage in their own version of cryptoglossia. However, twins have an advantage over other infants because, for them, cryptoglossia is a verbal bridge which they began constructing long before birth. You can imagine that twins must have had some way of letting each other know their needs in that shared womb. Their way of communicating was unique to their universe, which consisted entirely of each other (not counting mom). The result is that twins have no special need for interpreters, as they are accustomed to dealing with each other in a way that they can easily understand. For most twins, this is a way to "talk" with each other before having the benefit of a formalized language.

On rare occasions, the baby twinspeak communication pattern can go too far. In *The Silent Twins*, Marjorie Wallace reveals the life of twin girls who developed and mastered their own fast-paced language. Tragically, these twins withdrew into their twinship, and for most of their lives, treated the rest of the world (with few exceptions) to their silence, relating only to each other.

Fortunately, it is much more common for twins to outgrow their dependency on a secret childhood language. Still, those first crystal moments of information exchange between twins have a profound, lifelong effect. When we explored our communication challenges, we discovered that our baby twinspeak was quite powerful in setting the stage for our adult interaction styles.

THE TWIN TRAP FOR FAMILY MEMBERS

As baby twinspeak develops, it becomes an effective communication tool for the twins themselves. However, it is not so meaningful for those outside of the twinship. Predictably, the first problems encountered with twinspeak are within the family. That certain twin habit of dealing with each other in an effortless, seemingly off-handed manner seems natural to twins because they are growing and learning simultaneously. For us, our twinspeak style of fierce disagreements and sudden make-ups, which we developed very early on, did not work well with others—even within our family.

What would generally begin as a problem between the two of us would escalate to affect the entire family. When we had disagreements, they could be rather intense—complete with subversive attempts to champion other members of the family to support one twin over the other. The unsuspecting sibling might be swayed to take sides in the fray, only to find out that we had kissed and made up in the interim. Just as with our infantile disputes, our arguments would end for us as suddenly as they began, leaving the astonished sibling feeling confused and always appearing to be a traitor to at least one twin.

A nontwin can never really be in a win-win situation in the middle of a twinship. Our older sisters knew to steer clear of us when we were mad at each other. They learned that avoidance was the best way to evade capture in our twinspeak communication web. Unwittingly, our style was often influential in setting the tone for the family. Our oldest sister Terri condenses this thought into a single statement: "As the twins go, so goes the world."

United We Stand

As a result of twinspeak, it's common for twins to be united as one within their families. Twins' incredibly well-developed patterns of interaction help to establish an undying loyalty to one another. Many sets of twins have revealed to us how they often feel misunderstood in their families.

One fraternal twin, Suzanne, noticed that she has a

particular penchant for adamantly defending her twin brother, even against her husband. "When this happens, I can sense my husband's slowly seething resentment," Suzanne recalled. Defense of one's twin is instinctive in the twin bond. However, what comes automatically for a twin is too frequently viewed as betrayal by others.

Fraternal twins Joy and Jennifer have a similar problem with Jennifer's husband. Joy revealed, "My brother-in-law is very jealous of our relationship. There's a part of him that's unable to understand how close Jen and I are." These twins find this attitude perplexing, especially in light of the fact that this man's mother is an identical twin!

It is understandable how spouses could be frustrated with twinship—after all, they're coming into a well-established, tight relationship. But amazingly, we found that even some mothers of twins can have a hard time accepting their twins' closeness. Kari and Shari spoke of their mother's insecurity about their twin relationship. It seems their mother wanted to share the bond of these fraternal twins. When the twins gravitated exclusively to each other, the mother's disappointment would be obvious. Shari summarized it simply, "Our twinship divided our family." This split seems to occur most often if there is one or more family members who have strong, unexamined feelings of jealousy about the twins.

For instance, identical twin Gina sadly described her own mother's feelings over the attention she and her twin sister received. "Our mother was actually jealous of the time our father gave to us. She felt he was over-indulgent with us and lavished us with too much affection."

Gina and Tina were china-doll little girls. They were extremely close, with a communication style all their own. Their twinspeak only added to their mother's feeling of isolation from the twinship. You can just imagine the difficulties that arose in this family as these twins grew into beautiful young women.

It seems that no one is immune from feeling left out of the twin bond. No matter how close you are to twins, their ways of being with each other frequently seem confusing and overwhelming. However, in general, family members usually adapt on some level to the peculiarities of life with twins.

We were fortunate that our family adjusted to our twinspeak and, for the most part, learned to accept and/or ignore it. In this way, they evaded issues that can be the source of long-lasting family problems. This adaptation by our family, however, was a mixed blessing. It enabled our twinspeak to flourish but did not truly help us learn to communicate in the nontwin world.

THE EVOLUTION OF TWINSPEAK

Twinspeak is actually a combination of many communication techniques. These "twin ways" of conversing within the twinship are not typical of the general population, but each one adds to the complexity of twinspeak for nontwins, and sometimes for twins themselves.

Speaking and Thinking in Stereo

One frequent, obvious display of twinspeak is that of synchronized speech. Twins have told us numerous tales of finishing each other's sentences or saying the same word at the same time. In our family, this trait was appropriately dubbed "speaking in stereo." Such moments were highlighted with delightful peals of laughter—as if we had intentionally made it happen. This accidental activity shows how closely twin minds are joined.

Likewise, twins can also voice the same thought at *different* times. Nontwins tell of hearing the same phrases from each twin on separate occasions. A mutual friend of ours recently announced, "I'm starting to get over being surprised at hearing the exact same words from both of you. I think from now on, I'll only ask one of you what I need to know, since I'm going to get the same answer anyway!"

Even we were astonished during our survey process to see how many twins expressed the same thought in the same way—during segregated interview sessions. For example, Besse and Esther both told us that they could "read each other's mind." And Earl and Gearl both described their twinship with these words: "Neither of us is dominant; we both have a caring disposition." Why these simultaneous thoughts and expressions occur is a mystery. They certainly happen on occasion among siblings and friends, yet with twins these experiences are common occurrences. Whether fraternal or identical, twins are strongly connected and declare their bond with their not-so-coincidental "double-talk."

No Need for Words

Another fascinating element of twinspeak is nonverbal communication. Based on information exchange that begins *in utero*, twins establish deep-seated mechanisms for interacting, both with and without words. Although as twins we have many moments of simultaneous speech, we also have a gift for wordless communication. Our older sister Brenda evaluates it this way: "Your communication was on a very different level. Most of the time, you didn't seem to need words. You just had a sense of what the other was thinking and feeling."

Twins have a great deal of nonverbal communication and often thoughts are transferred through simple gestures. A raised eyebrow can communicate volumes to one's twin! This remarkable behavior appears to be the rule rather than the exception among twins. Esther defined twin "nonspeak" like this: "We can understand each other by a look between us or a word which can express a whole thought." Her identical twin, Besse, in a separate interview felt the same way. "We understand each other without having to use words."

Esther and Besse are in their early 80s and say that the need for words between them gets less and less as they grow older and closer. Interestingly, they are both widows, so now they spend a great deal of their time together. (Though as you will see later, these ladies have never really been separated for any significant amount of time.) Their closeness supports our findings that the twin bond, with its special communication patterns, naturally deepens over the years, especially when the twins live close enough to one another to share their lives on a daily basis.

The Twin Zone

Whether living in the same or different cities, twins

continue to be connected. Our research shows that the telephone lines are kept a-buzzing by twins. All the twins we interviewed thought about their twin *every day*. For those twins who are near each other, daily visits on the phone or in person are commonplace. Most separated twins communicate at least one to four times per week by phone. Twins just cannot seem to satisfy their need to communicate with each other.

From this constant contact to speaking in stereo and nonverbal communication, twins outwardly express their bond in what we call the "twin zone." As with other aspects of twinspeak, this activity grew out of twin interactions from infancy. Just as described by our uncle when we were babies, we are still definitely in our *own world*. Those who spend time around twins of all ages can sense this uncommon connection. However, as with other forms of twinspeak, trips to the twin zone can be disruptive to relationships outside of the twinship. What is only natural for twins due to the irresistible magnetism of the twin bond may appear downright rude to nontwins.

Therefore, nontwins are very aware of the twin zone. It is that special place only twins can go. (Sort of like, tick-tock-the-game-is-locked and nobody else can play!) The twin zone is a well-established way in which twins attach to their twinship. An unfortunate by-product of this space is that by virtue of going there, twins detach from others at the same time. Jennifer, a fraternal twin, acknowledged that her husband has always been especially keen to the way she and her twin sister isolate themselves. He told her, "When other people are in the room, you two tend to ignore them because you are on your own private wavelength."

The Twin Zone Is Unpredictable

The most intriguing aspect of the twin zone is the unconscious nature of it. Twins do not intentionally venture into the twin zone or premeditate the merger. When a trip to the twin zone will take place is just as much a mystery to twins as to nontwins. The conditions are highly favorable for twin zoning, however, when a good time between twins is in progress.

As adults, during our time of physical separation, when we were reunited, we would inadvertently end up merged together in the twin zone. We would simply be drawn to one another across the room, subconsciously maneuvering our positions until we were seated side-by-side on the couch, lost in conversation, and snugly wrapped in the comfort of our bond. This magnetic attraction typically dominated over other family matters and we were sometimes jokingly told to split up. (Mom would say, "Guess we're going to have to separate the twins!")

However, as with other forms of twinspeak, families of twins come to realize that twin-zoning is merely a part of life with twins. Our mom explains, "We know that every time you're together, you'll go off into some twin world of your own. We all basically ignore you because we know that you will eventually free yourselves from each other and come back to our reality when you're ready. We know we don't have any control over it—and guess that you don't either!"

Our family, like the families of most twins, can make light of twin-zone escape scenes because they are old-hat to them. In a sense, they know what to expect based strictly on memories of countless episodes with their twins over the years. However, those involved in new and continuing relationships with twins may find the experience a bit disconcerting. Amy, the wife of identical twin John, recalled, "Early in our relationship, I often felt left out when John's twin brother was around. This was a strange and uncomfortable feeling for me—like I was a third wheel." The feeling Amy was experiencing is odd to a significant other because normally they're used to being in the number one position in their mate's life.

Nancy's husband, Stu, is often subjected to our departures to our twin planet. The three of us spend a great deal of time together, which increases the likelihood that Stu will be left alone while we visit the twin zone. "It's as if you're enveloped in a bubble, floating off with each other into another universe," Stu describes.

The Twin Zone Is Not a Physical Departure

This twin zone separation, though not physical, is very apparent to nontwins. Stu says, "I feel a sense of isolation due to the air of exclusivity you drape around yourselves." At first, he reacted defensively to the situation. Understandably, his tendency to take the twin zone personally was in response to his insecurity with his new position in Nancy's life. A nontwin can genuinely feel hurt by the twin zone because they feel like they are being blatantly ignored.

Although twins' natural urge is to wall themselves off anyway, twins seem to truly zone out during relaxing, fun experiences. The closest, yet grossly inadequate, way to describe it is like an extremely private joke. For some reason, something one of us says will be deemed uncontrollably funny by the other one and our laughter will be the vehicle for sending us into the twin zone.

At these times, others may find the moment mildly humorous and are often surprised by what they see as an exceptional reaction by the twins. Most families of twins learn to accept this twin marvel with little more than a shrug and a shaking of the head.

The skill with which our family adapted to our twin zoning was both good and bad for us. Their calm understanding of it lessened our awareness of its impact on others.

To minimize the effects of the twin zone, twins must be cognizant of their isolationist tendencies. Their degree of exclusiveness can be metered to be inclusive of others. With time, we have grown to recognize the negative effect of our twin zone on others, especially Stu. We have consciously altered our propensity to float off together. This change has seemed to help reduce his feelings of being the odd man out. Our alertness to signs of his frustration has helped us expand the bubble to bring him into it (or at least limit the duration of our twin zone trips).

At the same time, nontwins can patiently grow to have some level of acceptance of the twin zone. Stu educated us on his adjustment, "I've had to learn to accept that you were oblivious to leaving me out of your conversations. I can see now that you didn't intend to exclude me; you were just caught up in your own world—your twin zone."

A Life with One Is a Life with the Other

Perhaps twins create the twin zone as a protective

measure to ensure security, or perhaps the zone is a natural extension of the twin bond. All the communication patterns outlined in this chapter stem from the remarkable closeness of twins in all aspects of their lives. The mysterious connection between the minds and souls of twins is captivating. Yet, this is the very trait that can become the barrier to twins' ability to relate to others outside of their twinship.

The strange truth for nontwins who have a relationship with a twin is that they are really involved with both twins (no matter how far apart the twins may live). It is virtually impossible for a twin to be separate from their twinship—just like it is impossible for anyone to disavow their race, background, birth order, etc. Being a twin colors your view of life. It is a part of who you are.

[*Nancy—It has taken years for Janna and me to discover that we are different people inside and outside of our twinship. But, suffice it to say for now that Stu obviously notices my behavior change when it comes to Janna. For one thing, I forget to let him know when she and I have made plans without first considering his schedule. And I often assume that I told him when I did not.*

Early in our marriage, Stu and I had an argument over the fact that I had chosen to spend time with Janna over him. He was exasperated with the situation and phoned a friend for a chance to vent. He spewed the story out to

Ron—complete with his frustration of always being in second place. Ron merely replied, "I don't know what you're so upset about. You're the one who married twins!"]

Ron had literally hit upon the heart of this issue. Twins are a vital part of each other's lives and the twinship is forever. There is no denying that fact.

This story is not meant to frighten nontwins away from forming relationships with twins, but rather to help them to remember that having a relationship with a twin is an experience different from having one with a nontwin. We believe that an education process is required to help both twins and nontwins realize the origins, influences, and consequences of twinspeak.

WHEN WORLDS COLLIDE: TWINSPEAK OUTSIDE THE TWINSHIP

Twins' versions of communicating are fascinating and comfortable inside the twinship. Unfortunately, they usually fall miserably short in the nontwin world. A fact of life for twins is that communication with someone who is not your twin requires the use of words. Learning such "foreign" skills is the challenge most twins face. On the flip side, understanding twins' innate communication tactics is the challenge nontwins face.

Twins exhibit twinspeak early in life, which follows

them into adulthood and consequently into other relationships. They tend to project their own twin communication styles into their nontwin relationships. Identical twin Rhonda explains, "Our habits of fighting, as well as our own ways of compromise, have come into all our other relationships."

Baby Twinspeak Grows Up

We expanded on our "forgive and forget" technique throughout our childhood and it evolved into a novel, yet mostly ineffective, communication strategy. For us, the pattern was: no matter how fierce the battle, within moments, forgiveness would prevail, smiles would return, and hugs would signal the end of a dispute. The details of what had transpired were not discussed, merely buried, as more important activities would take priority. We found that this behavior does not work well with others. (What a surprise!)

Though twin communication methods are custom-designed by each set of twins, we learned that our quick-to-fight-quick-to-make-up style is very common among twins. Denise, a fraternal twin, remembered that she and her twin brother fought often as children, even pushing each other during disagreements, but "these fights did not last long because we were each other's favorite playmate." It is understandable that this "quick make-up" technique is successful for twins because they must develop the right processes to make the twinship function. Twins do not have the time or energy to stay angry with each other for very long because they are *constantly together*. Their closeness would be unbearable otherwise.

Another style that seemed to be popular among the twins we researched was the "we don't fight" style. Some twins declare that they have never had a fight with their twin. We believe that this style is, deep down, very similar to ours, when reduced to its basics. Twins who refuse to fight with their twins merely jump to the forgiveness stage more readily. It is the quick-to-silence-quick-to-make-up strategy. This is just another way of fast (though probably not so thorough) dispute resolution which is necessary in the extreme closeness surrounding life lived as twins.

Tailoring Twinspeak

Clearly, twinspeak has to be tailored to some other communication style outside of the twinship since others cannot communicate in the same intense way that twins do. This can be difficult for twins by virtue of the fact that since childhood, their reality is that at least one person on the planet *can* frequently read their mind. Mike relates that his wife is constantly shocked at how little he and his identical twin brother actually speak to each other when they are together. "We don't really have to speak that much because we are comfortable just knowing what each other is thinking. Sometimes I say things and think to myself, 'Those were really Mark's words,'" Mike admitted.

Tried-and-true twinspeak, including twin non-speak, does not translate into a language with any meaning for nontwins. So twins must learn to make adjustments in their twinspeak. Our twin communication (or more often non-communication) method proved to be devastating in many of our adult relationships. Others did not naturally have the tolerance for the fast-paced abuse and instant release of disputes that we had grown accustomed to in our twin life. We now know that in the nontwin world, other people require more verbal expression combined with focused attention because they cannot "just get it and get over it" like we can with each other. We've had to learn the importance of conveying thoughts and feelings in real time.

Putting feelings into words was quite a challenge for us. Since we've shared so many years of indirect communication, dealing directly with one another (and others) was an odd and often uncomfortable feeling, at first. For instance, over the years, we've had numerous exasperated boyfriends cry out, "I cannot read your mind! I don't know what you expect of me." Our point of reference is, of course, each other. We know each other so well that indeed we *do* know what to expect from one another. It has taken many years and many aggravated friends for us to realize that we *have to* verbalize—*out loud*—our expectations of others to them.

Twins come to realize that quick release of conflict *without resolution* is fertile ground for resentment to grow, even within the twinship. As we matured, our coping skills remained frozen in time. We continued to easily forgive, as we had in childhood, but forgetting became more difficult. Consequently, the dreaded relationship tactic of "gunnysacking" unexpressed feelings became part of our communication bag of tricks. Instead of confronting issues, the hurt feelings are shoved into a gunnysack for storage. The end result is predictable—one day the gunnysack explodes all over your unsuspecting twin, partner, or friend. Often many months of uncommunicated issues come spewing forth. By this time, both people are so overwhelmed that resolution of any problem becomes unlikely.

The relationship difficulties that can arise from twinspeak can be avoided with awareness and understanding. We've formulated a list of tips for consideration by nontwins involved with twins, as well as for twins themselves. (As with other hints, they appear in

Appendix II.)

Twins foster a relationship style that makes life for them easier inside of their twinships. What happens when twins face the outside world? Well, most do well by conquering it as a team.

CHAPTER 5

TWO HEADS ARE BETTER THAN ONE

✴

When it came to dating, I was very shy and could hardly talk to girls. Earl was much more able to handle this. Together we were a better team in the dating game because I was more comfortable with him around.

—Gearl, 64-year-old identical twin

Growing up on a farm is hard work. But for us, doing our chores together was almost no effort since we just knew how each other worked.

—Earl, Gearl's twin

Build for your team a feeling of oneness,
of dependence on one another,
and of strength to be derived from unity.

—Vince Lombardi

✳

Two heads are better than one. It's an expression you've heard many times in your life. You have probably even experienced the feeling a time or two— like when someone comes along and puts the piece into the puzzle that you've spent hours searching for. Twins embody this age-old adage for they often work together as a team without even thinking about it.

We can all relate to times in our lives when teamwork resulted in a job well done and a mission successfully accomplished. Now imagine being so much in tune with your teammate that you work together without even thinking about it. Where your work stops, your teammate's work effortlessly begins. That begins to describe the teamwork of twins.

From the very beginning of life as twins, working together must be a priority. Twins are suspended together in an extremely small and cramped space. Harmony, and most likely even survival, depend upon learning to choreograph movements for co-existence.

For example, fraternal twins typically each have their own placenta which provides food from the mother's body to each of the babies. However, in one case we were told about, one of the babies' placentas had become detached and was no longer providing vital nutrition to that twin. Somehow, magically, the twins found a way for nutrients to go from the still-attached placenta to both babies. Though one of the twins was significantly smaller than his brother at birth, amazingly both survived. The truly remarkable part of the story is that the smaller twin was the one who had shared his lifeline with his brother.

BABY COLLABORATIONS

We have been told by many sets of twins about their methods of teamwork, even as small children. One overwhelming example, which also happens to be true in our lives, is the story of breaking out of the crib. In our case, our mother told us that when we were about eighteen months old, she was often perplexed to find us out of our cribs and playing, soon after she had put us down for a nap.

Mom knew that we hadn't fallen out of our cribs because we weren't injured in any way. One day she hid in the small closet in our room to try to discover our secret.

Nancy awoke first and sat up in her crib. She then crawled to the edge and adeptly tripped the latch so that the side of the crib came down far enough for her to climb over. (She was always a daredevil!) Once on the floor, she waddled to Janna's crib to awaken her. We would both undo the latch on the second crib— and *voilà*, escaped babies!

Similar stories hold true of most multiples. Parents

of sextuplets revealed in an interview that they cannot leave their six two-year-olds unattended for even one minute. The father reported, "These little guys have dismantled beds, taken doors off hinges, and completely turned over large pieces of furniture. When I hid to watch them, it was astounding to see how they worked together like a well-oiled piece of machinery, in unison and with great efficiency."

Rhonda suggested that working so well together as children was merely a function of being each other's favorite pastime. "As kids, my twin sister and I never had very many dolls or toys because we wouldn't play with them. We entertained ourselves with each other."

Our sister Brenda often saw this twin collaboration in action. "When you two were young, you did everything together," she recalls. "Your cooperation was especially obvious when you were creating something. The two of you would make up skits and dances together and then perform them for the neighborhood— usually giggling all the way. Your 'pairing up' tendency seemed to make all your chores and your lives all the merrier."

Socializing

Teaming up also affects the socialization of twins. There are two of you to face the world. Oddly enough, in the social arena, twinship can be both helpful and challenging.

At the sensitive age of 14, we were thrust into a new school in a new town. We faced the unknown together, as we embarked upon our first day at Evans Junior High School in Lubbock, Texas. Our twinship proved to be a great icebreaker. Obstacles to meeting new people melt away pretty easily when someone walks up to you and says, "Are you a twin? I was wondering why that girl in my first period class kept changing clothes so many times during the day!" The two of us covered more territory and brought more people into our circle due to our twinship.

Likewise, Andrea felt that her twin brother was a tremendous positive influence on her social development. "I think Vince has really helped my understanding of the opposite sex," she told us. He taught her how males succeed in life—things such as how men use aggressiveness and competitiveness in their approach to life's problems. Vince, on the other hand, explained to us that Andrea showed him the "feeling" side of life. He credited her for his development of sensitivity.

Although twins can use twinship to enhance their circle of friends, ironically it can also cause them to have fewer friends. That cozy feeling twins have with one another can lull them into a sense of complacency when it comes to venturing out for social interactions.

Sometimes it's hard to find the delicate balance between comfort with each other and inclusion of others.

Shari experienced this painful reality with her twin sister. When she and Kari were children, Shari was surprised to learn that Kari was not always going to be included in social events, just because she was Shari's twin. With Shari's outgoing personality, she was naturally popular at school, while Kari's shy nature made her reclusive. The inevitable was bound to happen. Shari got invited to parties, while Kari did not. Shari was left with an extremely difficult choice—her friends or her twin.

Shari finally had to decide to leave Kari behind, despite knowing that the choice would be hurtful. "During those days, we used to fight a lot," she lamented. "Kari did not make any effort for herself to establish outside friendships and relied on me for that. I was always so relieved when Kari was also invited to parties. That made it so much easier for me." When Kari wasn't invited the result was negative for them both: Kari had feelings of abandonment, Shari feelings of guilt. Kari also remembered those times, "Shari's friends were very outgoing. I really didn't feel part of them—or her, either, when she was with them."

Not all twins are as polar in their introverted/extroverted tendencies as Shari and Kari. Yet, other twins' comfort with one another can still interfere with their ability and desire to meet others. Cathy decided many years ago, "My twin and I are loners. We don't have any close friends. I'm not good at making friends, because I never needed to since I always had a best friend. I know that my social skills are lacking. I can't just pick up the phone and call anyone. I've always had that comfort zone with Chris." Chris concurred. "Cathy is my best friend, and therefore, regardless of my feelings for a friend, I remain more loyal to my twin. I consciously choose her company over others, and consequently, I have shut out a lot of people."

TWINS AND ENTREPRENEURSHIP

As their socialization process continues, twins grow accustomed to being with each other. Whether they easily make friends outside of their twinship or not, the security they find in being together is a reinforcement of the twin bond. This support translates into a remarkable ability to work well together.

Twins simply have an uncanny way of bringing out the best in each other. Lisa and Debbie Ganz are part-owners of Twins Restaurant in Manhattan (and soon to be in Los Angeles). This eatery is staffed by many sets of identical twins. Seeing double there has nothing to do with having too many cocktails! The twin atmosphere is so important that if one twin calls in sick, the owners request that the other twin stay home also.

Other examples of twins choosing the same work are Harvey and Horace Grant who are nearly-seven-foot-tall, professional basketball players. Identical twins Albert and Allen Hughes are up-and-coming directors in Hollywood. Their first popular film was "Menace II Society." And Mary-Kate and Ashley Olsen began early careers as actresses and models, getting their start as stand-ins for each other on the television sit-com "Full House."

Our Journey to One Place

While many twins head in the same career direction as they grow, others take a fork in the road and head in opposite directions. We fit into the latter category, at least for a few turns down the road of life. Our story demonstrates the power of two heads and the results that can be created by them.

We started college at age 17. Nancy was very much drawn to science and math, while Janna's fancy turned more to literature and psychology. Though we lived together and took many of the same courses at first, we were not really very interested in each other's lives during those years.

Our twin bond had been very strong all of our lives. But now, we were on a desperate search for our own identities. Like all teenagers, finding ourselves became our paramount mission in life. However, it was strange for us because our lives had been shared so closely up until this point. As our search for our own identities progressed, our twinship slowly drifted apart.

Looking back, it was unusual for us to not be in tune with one another. The movement away from each other was subtle (and natural for our development). But we'd always worked well together. Nevertheless, at that time, all we knew was that we were antagonistically working against each other.

Nancy had decided at the tender age of 15 years that she wanted to pursue a career in medical research. That was the year that our father died of colon cancer, after many long months of suffering. Nancy found motivation and inspiration to work toward a cure to end that kind of pain for families. Janna was more interested in talking with people and helping to resolve problems. She saw a need for more honesty and communication within families, especially during times of crisis and despair.

So off we ventured: Nancy toward science and math; Janna toward family relations and psychology. This split in our academic interests was shortly followed by a division of our home.

During our second year of college, Nancy started living only a few blocks away; however, this move was a huge event in our lives. We never realized the adjust-ment that lurked behind those brown, U-Haul boxes that contained all of Nancy's separate belongings. Waiting there in the darkness were issues for us to un-pack. It would take almost two decades before we got to that job.

Living apart, we had to learn to be on our own for the first time, even though we had been away from home for over two years. For singletons, learning to be on your own means moving away from mom and dad; for us, it meant moving away from each other. It was very bizarre to go to bed for the first time without each other being in the house.

Nancy completed her undergraduate degree, ob-tained her medical technology certification, and then entered into graduate school to begin work on her Ph.D. in cellular and molecular biology—her road to researching cancer. Janna received her undergraduate degree in family relations and began working at vari-ous jobs, mostly *un*related to the helping professions. Finally, Janna took a job as a legal assistant which sparked her desire to be a different type of counselor.

Nancy's education eventually took her through graduate school and on to a post-doctoral position at Vanderbilt University in Nashville, Tennessee. Janna continued to work in Midland, Texas, while gaining interest in a legal career. By now, we'd been apart for several years and that trend would linger for almost 17 years before we would come to live together again in the same place.

We spoke very often on the telephone. We still joke that it would have been cheaper for us to have lived together in those days than to have paid those phone bills. Our talks were our forum for two-headed problem solving. We would each present our life's issues and collaborate on a resolution. The true feeling of our twin bond really came through for us during those years. In fact, it was during one of our lengthy phone conversations that Nancy "inspired" Janna to finally go ahead and enroll in law school. She casually asked, "So how is your wasted potential today? Don't you want to do something more with your life?" Although her tone was joking, we both knew that the time was right. So, in the late '80s, Nancy finished her graduate work and Janna began hers.

We had great plans to live together in Dallas, Texas: Janna practicing law at a large law firm and Nancy continuing her research at Baylor Medical Center. We dreamed of living together with endless time to chat and make plans. We knew that every time we put our heads together to solve a problem, the answer came quickly and easily. We wanted that benefit in our daily lives. Well, let's just say, our plans were interrupted. Isn't it wonderful how the universe will sometimes alter your plans and move you in another direction? That's what happened to us.

Although Janna did move to Dallas, employed by a large law firm, Nancy received an offer she couldn't refuse to move to San Diego, California, as a research scientist with a new biotechnology company.

At that time, biotechnology was the up-and-coming industry on the west coast. It's still a booming field which invites great creativity from many different professions. As it turns out, two of these just so happen to be science and law.

After Nancy's move to San Diego, we grew increasingly tired of our separation. Janna was easily lured into making her own move to San Diego. Have you ever been there? If so, you know how beautiful and enticing it is. This was one of life's no-brainer choices: being together as twins and living in San Diego. We're reminded of the words in Garth Brooks' popular country song, "Some of God's greatest gifts are unanswered prayers." We didn't make that date where we planned to reunite in Dallas; however, our long-awaited reunion was even better on the west coast!

Once Janna's job search began in San Diego, it became obvious to us that the biotechnology industry was an even hotter area for lawyers than we'd anticipated—especially ones who also had a Ph.D. in science. We used to kid each other that if we were one person, with our combined J.D. and Ph.D., we would be an extremely marketable commodity. We had no idea just how prophetic that statement would turn out to be.

[Janna—*My career as a litigator led me from the large law firm atmosphere to a very small, six-lawyer firm. Though the work was exciting and stimulating, I was painfully unhappy with it. In late 1992, when I had just finished trying a three-month trial in federal court with one of the firm's founding partners, I reached an all-time low. My work was no longer fulfilling. I was so depressed that I could hardly manage to drag myself out of bed every day to go into the office. Obviously, it was time for me to do something else with my life. The signals from the universe were loud and clear.*]

[Nancy—*At this time, my career was quite satisfying. I was enjoying the transition from an academic researcher to an industry scientist. Almost daily, I gained new insights into pharmaceutical product development which allowed me to apply my science skills in the business world.*]

Nancy's enthusiasm for her work was like a neon sign that read: "You really have to love your job in order to appreciate life." Fortunately, Janna saw the light.

Dreams Do Come True

One evening Janna's roommate casually commented,

"Hey, look at this want ad. It sounds just like you." It was an ad in the Help Wanted section for a contract lawyer for the medical school of a local university.

[*Janna—I took the paper from her with some trepidation; however, once I read the ad, I instantly had a feeling that this job would be my refuge, my escape. And it was.*

The position brought me into the healthcare field where I learned a great deal about science and medicine. Now, at last, I could speak and understand the language of Nancy's career. Our conversations became sprinkled with comments on cell biology, NIH grants, project timelines, and FDA approvals of clinical trials and products. Little did we know that we were rehearsing for a life-changing experience.

As I became more and more educated on the legal aspects of healthcare and biotechnology, an unbelievable opportunity opened up for me to become an in-house attorney for a growing biotechnology company. This opportunity was no coincidence.

I had negotiated the university's position with this company for a contract between the company and the university. The negotiations had been very painless—mostly because I didn't have to deal with a lawyer for the company. At that time, the company was without a lawyer on staff. I told my contact at the company that they really needed a lawyer to make my job at the university more challenging during contract negotiations. Several months later, I became that lawyer.]

In the meantime, the biotech company that had re-
cruited and promoted Nancy had fallen on hard times.

*[Nancy—The company's predominant clinical study
failed. That event led to bankruptcy. It was difficult because I was one of the few employees who remained after
the ordeal. Though I had gained valuable knowledge in
both company start-ups and, now, company wind-downs,
this job had definitely lost its luster. But, my excitement
about the biotech industry had not waned. I got busy putting
my curriculum vitae together for my impending job search.]*

When the employment recruiter at the company
where Janna was newly employed got wind that her
identical twin sister (who was still at a competing company) was in the job market, his ears literally perked
up. To make a long story short, the company reviewed
Nancy's c. v., interviewed her thoroughly yet speedily,
and four short months to the day after Janna started
working at the company, Nancy showed up for her
first day on the job as project director of the company's
cartilage research program. It's not exactly curing cancer, but it is making a significant difference in the quality of people's lives!

Though we no longer work there, that opportunity
was truly a dream come true for us. As far as we knew,
we were the only identical twins employed by the same
company in that industry. We got to see each other
every day and even worked together on many projects.

This experience taught us that the power of our twinship was not simply additive. An exponential synergy results when we combine our efforts to solve a problem. We've come to call our two heads working together "twinergy."

In fact, we used to get a kick out of confusing fellow co-workers. Once they got us mixed up, it was very difficult for them to ever get us straightened out again. Once a woman came to Nancy's office and proceeded to go into great detail about an agreement that she needed. Nancy had to finally interrupt her and redirect her to the legal department. She still had a problem getting us sorted out and called on Nancy two more times about that agreement before she got us straight.

Another time, Nancy had given a company-wide presentation. The following day, a young employee came up to Janna and touted Nancy's performance. Janna listened patiently and kindly informed him that she would pass his feedback on to Nancy. He blushed and stated, "You two sure look a lot alike after your latest haircut." (Ah, that old "new haircut" excuse . . .)

You simply cannot imagine how powerful the experience of working together is for us. Those shared biotech jobs were a training ground for our new lives. We now spend the days together working on our own dreams. Our combined thoughts and faith made it happen. NEVER give up on your dreams. They do come true.

Other Career Path Crossings

Besse and Esther have let their two heads create a similar experience for them. While they were growing up, they noticed and cultivated a shared love for music. Their home contained twin pianos where the girls practiced together daily. Besse related, "We studied endless hours, notes from our pianos filling the house [and probably the neighborhood] with music. This dedication led us to careers as duo-pianists." The love and comfort they found in playing together as children developed into satisfying careers.

John and Walt know this feeling on another level. They both work in the social services field. John is a lawyer and employed by the county to provide family services, especially in the representation of children who are in need of a safe home. Walt has a master's degree in public health and provides social services for the Asian community. "It's interesting that our careers have taken very similar paths," Walt said. "It's even better that these paths often cross since John works a great deal with social workers in the area." Sometimes John's recommendations for his clients' foster care will result in children being placed in homes where Walt has counseled. John added, "We share a great feeling of making a real difference in the community."

Twins naturally make great teammates. Gearl and Earl knew this. They played on the same football team and were known as "Double Trouble" for their coordinated efforts on the field. In fact, twins are the ultimate team—embodying unity and dependence upon one another. Twin teamwork is like having four arms and four legs to tackle physical tasks, and one brain and one heart to put into all tasks. Often the heart connection is the strongest attribute of all. It can carry twins through even the most difficult problem.

THE COOPERATIVE SPIRIT OF HEALING

We cannot think of a better example of two heads being better than one than the story of Kathy and Karen. Their story is one of enormous heart.

Kathy and Karen were born on November 17, 1958, in Blue Bell, Pennsylvania. They've been extremely close all their lives, but didn't ever *really* know whether they were identical or fraternal twins. It never mattered to them what kind of twins they were—just that they had each other. Theirs was a life filled with sharing.

In high school, they shared an interest in field hockey. In college, they shared the same major, the same love for skiing, the same house, and an almost identical ranking in their graduating class—finishing one after the other in academic ranking. Their bond didn't need to be defined by society's standards. They were quite comfortable having their twin relationship as they defined it for themselves.

In January 1996, Kathy and Karen's comfort was suddenly shattered. Kathy was diagnosed with multiple myeloma, a rare and untreatable form of blood cancer. What type of twins they were (fraternal or identical) now took on a real and sobering importance: having an identical twin could greatly impact Kathy's chances of obtaining the most advanced treatments for her disease, including bone marrow transplants. Tests revealed that Kathy and Karen are indeed identical twins. They are genetic duplicates of one another. Karen's bone marrow is an exact match for Kathy's. When the time is appropriate, both women will undergo a procedure in an attempt to save Kathy's life.

Kathy and Karen have become a team to fight this battle. Kathy recounted the moment she was told the devastating news:

"I was driving down the highway and returned my doctor's call on my cellular telephone. He told me that blood tests, which had been run to help my husband and me determine why we were having trouble conceiving our second child, showed that I had this rare form of cancer. The next morning was Saturday and I went with my husband to see my doctor.

"My husband is a wonderful man and I could not love him more than I do, but I so desperately needed to talk to Karen. I knew a burden would be lifted just by talking to her. I called her when we got home. It was such a relief to know that the pain was being shared, that I had another back-bone." Karen depicted that telephone call as "an unforgettable, vivid moment." She told us:

"I had been out running errands—all concerned about the new tile for our home remodel. When the phone rang, it was Kathy. She said my name in a voice that was so tiny. It was a voice I had never heard before.

"She told me that she had cancer. I went numb. This put everything in my life suddenly in perspective for me. How could I be bothered and upset over tile? Now, I knew what really mattered in my life."

Though they were living in separate cities at the time, Kathy and Karen spent countless hours collaborating on how to attack this problem. They are self-professed analytics (Kathy has an MBA from Harvard and is an executive director of a large pharmaceutical company, while Karen is an attorney with a major publishing company). Their approach to the disease is a well-developed, highly-organized game plan which involves everything from creating a nonprofit foundation to increase research and educational efforts about this disease to their actual participation in experimental research.

As Kathy and Karen stressed their analytical strategy to attack their current situation, we could not help but notice the "twin" approach that was unfolding as well. You could hear a gentleness come to their voices as they described their feelings about each other and the disease.

Kathy's life is dramatically changed forever. She is steadfast in her belief, however, that the most important move she can make now is a move to the city where Karen lives. Kathy's husband is completely supportive of this idea. He told Kathy that he can see that she is the most at peace and content when she is near Karen. Kathy declared, "I know that my life is one with Karen's."

Karen tries every moment to put herself in Kathy's place. She disclosed to us, "I pointedly ask myself what I would want if I were in Kathy's shoes. The answer is always honesty." So she provides an honest, loving net for Kathy to fall into every day. Both women are excitedly looking forward to the day, soon, when this support can be provided in person, when Kathy moves to Karen's city.

Kathy and Karen both admit to feeling somewhat

helpless. However, neither of them showed us any signals of feeling out of control. Kathy proclaimed, "I am stronger because I know that I am not alone since Karen is right here in my heart." While Karen simply summed up her feelings by stating, "Kathy is me and I am her."

These twins' cooperation in the act of healing is remarkable. Their two heads and one intermingled heart truly show the power of twinship. Kathy's disease is "smoldering" and Karen continues to wait, knowing she may be called on to provide a much more active role in Kathy's treatment as a bone marrow donor. When that time comes, we know these twins will be ready as a team to face that healing challenge.

A twinship is a training exercise in teamwork and collaboration. This skill has many benefits for the twinship and other relationships, as well. Perhaps all this working together creates the fertile ground that twins need to further cultivate their bond, a bond that is often surrounded by mystery and coincidence—what we have come to know as "twincidence."

CHAPTER 6

TWINCIDENCE

✸

We are in "contact" with each other even when we aren't together. It's that feeling everyone has from time to time, when you are able to notice the significance of an experience instantly while it is happening - with my twin I have a low-level sensation of this feeling all the time.

—Vince, 32-year-old fraternal twin

Vince and I are kindred spirits. We have shared so much and know each other so well that we are just in sync. It's a feeling of being together, even when we are apart.

—Andrea, Vince's twin

Coincidence is God's way of performing a miracle anonymously.

—Unknown

Gary, a fraternal twin, had disagreed with his brother about the Viet Nam war. Gary stayed in school, while Mark decided to go serve his tour of duty. Tragically, Mark was killed in Viet Nam. "I was out with a friend of mine and I knew something bad had happened to Mark," Gary laments. "I told my friend that I could just feel that he was dead. The phone call came the next day."

How did Gary "know" that something had happened to Mark? Are twins supernatural? Do they feel each other's pain? Can twins sense their twin's sensations? Can twins read each other's thoughts?

We can't say whether twins *really* have telepathic powers or if there is merely an increased awareness of each other due to their intimacy. But twins do seem to have some grander link connecting them that transcends mere happenstance. However you look at it, twins definitely have a mystical side that is filled with coincidence—or for us, "twincidence."

A SENSE OF EACH OTHER

Twins just seem to *know* what is happening with their twins. This "knowing" is beyond concrete thought and the senses. It's a type of twincidence that is based on a "sixth" sense, a shared consciousness of each other.

Psychic phenomena, such as premonitions, visions,

and strong gut feelings, have allured and frustrated humankind for centuries. There doesn't appear to be an apparent answer for their cause or origin. As a result, many have doubted the validity of psychic experiences—mostly due to the fact that these incidents occur spontaneously. Skeptics argue that because such experiences do not readily lend themselves to repetition in an experimental setting, they do not exist in any meaningful way. Such occurrences seemingly defy the laws of science.

It is true that extrasensory perception, telepathy, mind-reading, clairvoyance, and the like are not tangible things. You cannot touch them; you cannot see them; you cannot even replicate or manipulate them. But they do exist. We found them to be quite apparent in the lives of twins.

The existence of psychic events is beyond our five senses. It is beyond the grasp of our pure physical world. But let's not be so limiting in our reality. Just because you have never seen, touched, smelled, heard, or tasted a *thought* or *feeling* does not mean that you question their existence. So it goes with psychic phenomena.

Tuned In on the Same Wavelength

A step into the lives of twins will show how the unexplained experience of twincidence just seems to follow them around. Twins do not intentionally try to be on the same wavelength as their twins. It happens naturally and without effort.

For example, several twins reported to us the experience of *knowing* when their twins were telephoning them. Jennifer, a fraternal twin, said that no matter how much time passes between telephone calls with her sister, there are many occasions "when the phone rings and I just know that it's Joy . . . I'm always right." Joy added, "We often get busy signals from calling each other at exactly the same time."

Of course, these types of events can take place in the lives of other family members and friends. However, they appear to occur more frequently with twins. Renee said it this way, "We often *know* when the other is down and not feeling well. It's a matter of simply knowing that each other is upset or out of balance. We are very much in tune that way." Vince put it in perspective by saying, "I just have stronger—what I guess I will call feelings—for and about my twin, both good and bad. I have a real sense of our uniqueness."

Twins' patterns of being tuned in to each other allow them to be even more intensely aware of each other's feelings. One vivid example of the ability of twins to tune into one another can be observed during the playing of games. It didn't take long for family and friends to catch on to the unfair advantage we had in a friendly game of Pictionary®. As a result, we were ultimately banned from being on the same team. Was it our fault that when one of us drew a line, the other one saw a tree? Not coincidentally, this same story has been told to us by families and friends of other twins. Forced separation of the twins seems to be the only way to level the playing field for parlor games.

Besse and Esther have an intensely close relationship. "We have even written letters to each other, at the same time, conveying the same thoughts, and magically, have had those letters cross each other in the mail," Esther recalled. Interestingly, Besse told us the same story in a separate survey answered without her sister. (Another twincidence?)

Cathy clarified it for us: "My twin and I have psychic experiences every time we're together! It's everything from knowing what the other is going to say to showing up in the same outfit."

We think of it as a kind of mind-melding (to borrow from Mr. Spock of "Star Trek"). Though it may have a genetic component, perhaps it stems more from a shared core value system, coupled with literally growing up and developing at exactly the same time. In other words, twins have simultaneous lives.

Twins simply know each other *so* well. You've probably encountered a couple who has been married for 30 or 40 years. You surely have observed them responding the same to situations or appearing to read each other's minds. They have developed a strong magnetism between them that breeds an uncanny ability to communicate nonverbally. So it is with twins. They merely have a jump start on this type of familiarity—their closeness begins at conception.

FEELING EACH OTHER'S PAIN

The connection twins have for each other can escalate to an even higher level. Practically all of the twins we researched, fraternal and identical alike, report that they've felt each other's pain or have had a sense of foreboding about their twin.

As children we were inseparable; however, our personalities were quite different.

[Janna—*In my role as the caregiver of the twins, I oozed sensitivity. Nancy was a little more carefree and able to quickly bounce back from the childhood bumps and scrapes that would leave me running to Mom for comfort. What became apparent as we grew older was that I would often feel Nancy's pain.*

One day we were at our Grandma and Grandpa's house in Fritch, Texas. The front door of their old house was a cold, metal-frame storm door. It contained a double-paned window that slid up and latched open to let the rare, dry breeze blow through the house. On this particular Sunday after our huge lunch, Grandpa had opened that storm door window to stave off the late afternoon sun while the adults sat back to lazily digest. We kids took advantage of the opportunity to run in and out of the house as we played. The old latch on that window began to loosen from all the activity. We were about six years old and were blissfully unaware of the danger that lurked above that open window.

Nancy was inside the house watching as a game of tag escalated among the cousins. When she innocently placed her hands on that window sill, the latch unexpectedly released and the window suddenly slammed down on her right hand. Shock and pain swept through her as blood started to flow from the tiny trapped hand. Before Nancy could even let out a scream, I came running up on the porch and began to drown out her fear with my own shrieking. Nancy swayed back and forth while enormous tears streamed down both of our faces.

Our Uncle Roland was the first adult on the scene. He quickly and expertly rescued Nancy's hand from its window prison. "I remember having to gather both of you up in my arms to comfort and calm you," he recounts. "If I hadn't been right there and seen for myself who was hurt, I wouldn't have been able to tell, because you were both screaming so loudly." Long after Nancy's hand was washed and bandaged, I stayed upset, clinging to her for dear life. Everyone there agrees that I genuinely felt Nancy's pain on that day.

This "pain-sharing" has only been strengthened and re-affirmed as we have grown into our adult lives. Recently, Nancy had surgery to remove an enlarged cyst below her left knee. Immediately after the surgery, I noticed a sharp, piercing pain below my left knee. I had never been injured there, nor had I ever noticed pain in that area before that day. It took several days for us to realize that I was again feeling Nancy's pain. I started to rub my knee subconsciously and tell Nancy, "Hurry up and heal!" As mysterious as it began, the pain ended for me once Nancy's rehabilitation was complete. Somehow I just need to figure out a way to keep Nancy from hurting herself and causing both of us pain!]

Several sets of female identical twins have amazed us by describing how they've felt each other's childbirth labor pains. Josephine explained, "When I went into labor with my first child, Fran had severe pain also. Although she was also pregnant, she wasn't due for another six months. Then, when she gave birth later that year, I felt her labor even though I was miles away and wasn't even aware that she'd gone to the hospital to have her baby." Fran was quick to add, "I still feel my sister's pain and suffering from time to time since that experience."

Similarly, Esther felt Besse's pain when Besse gave birth to her son. "I somehow felt the labor pains of

Besse's very difficult and intense delivery, though we were separated by many miles," she told us.

SOMETHING HAS HAPPENED . . .

This *sense* of each other can also be expressed through a feeling or foreboding that your twin is in trouble or is hurt. These events are clairvoyant in nature. Like Gary's story of feeling the death of his twin, other twins have reported to us that they can have a mysterious impulse about the health of their twins. It seems as though twins have a shared spirit which masquerades in the external world as psychic ability.

John remembered that when he and his twin brother James were adolescents, James was riding a mini-bike with friends in a vacant field. John was sitting at home on the front porch talking with his mother. Their mother recalled, "John stopped in the middle of a sentence, went white as a ghost and bluntly exclaimed, 'Something has happened to James. He's really hurt.'" Within minutes a neighbor ran up to them hysterically, saying that James had mangled his arm in an accident on the mini-bike. John had just *known* that James was hurt. "It was an overwhelming feeling that gripped my soul," he explained.

Chris didn't exactly describe her feelings about her twin sister's accident as a psychic experience. However, we can't help but see it that way. While traveling in Europe, Chris's sister, Cathy, was involved in a major traffic accident. Chris relived that day for us: "I had this nagging urge to call my sister over and over again. The feeling was an urgent, almost desperate, need to connect with Cathy." The need was not settled until she finally reached Cathy. Though she learned of the accident at that time, Chris was relieved to find out that Cathy was not badly injured.

This "sense" of your twin can even survive death. Elvis Presley was born with a twin brother, Jesse, who was stillborn. Doctors believed, and told the family, that Jesse died as a result of being strangled by Elvis's umbilical chord.

During childhood, after Elvis learned of his brother's bizarre death, family members say he never seemed to stop grieving the loss. Those closest to Elvis remember that before almost every live performance, he would state: "It's going to be okay; Jesse is on the stage with me."

This seeming extrasensory perception of twins can't be accounted for scientifically, or even logically, for that matter. Some twins experience it more than others and some report that they have not experienced it at all. We think it's really a case of heightened awareness.

From our research, the twins who informed us that

they didn't feel that they'd had "psychic" experiences also told us that they often shared the same thoughts at the same time and often finished each other's sentences. Hmm?! Seems pretty psychic to us. We challenge twins to start paying closer attention to those feelings, sensations, and intuitions that are shared with their twins—such flashes are probably signaling a connection with their twins that has yet to be harnessed and cultivated. Personally, once we started looking for twincidences in our lives, they magically appeared, practically around every corner.

ACCIDENT OR NOT?

As compelling as the twin *psychic* phenomenon is, we discovered an equally astonishing number of physical coincidences that have occurred between twins. This fact was not surprising to us for, if you think about it, the mere existence of twins as twins is the ultimate physical twincidence.

The Coincidence of Twincidence

Ah, coincidence, another difficult concept to accept. *Webster's New Collegiate Dictionary* defines *coincidence* as: "The occurrence of events that happen at the same time by accident but seem to have some connection."

Chance is defined as: "Something that happens unpredictably without discernible human intention or observable cause." It has been said that all coincidences are meaningful—that is certainly true of the creation of twins!

We humans unknowingly welcome supernatural events—without even trying. We've all had times or coincidences in our lives that could be considered psychic if we took a closer look at them.

What about those dreams that actually do come true, or that intense feeling that something is going to happen and it proves to be accurate? A very common experience that we all speak of regularly is that good old feeling of *déjà vu*. Or, have you ever had a strong, intuitive inclination to go in one direction when your rational mind was directing you in another? Have you ever looked to your heart for an answer and found it there? Has opportunity ever knocked? Haven't you had a lucky day? Ever been in the right place at the right time? What about an extraordinary coincidence that simply cannot be easily dismissed—you know, a coincidence so overpowering that it *can't* possibly be coincidental?

Perhaps a look at how others have viewed coincidence will be helpful. The Swiss psychologist Carl Jung spent much of his career studying and contemplating coincidence. He coined the term "synchronicity" to describe meaningful coincidences that do not have an apparent cause. Philosopher Arthur Schopenhauer believed in coincidences but characterized them as having a real significance only to those involved since, for others, the event would simply pass unnoticed into the background of life.

Since the time of Jung and Schopenhauer, others have taken a more liberal approach, suggesting that we do have some participation in the coincidences of our lives. In fact, many view such events as having great meaning for all of us.

The reluctant messiah, Donald Shimoda, in Richard Bach's tremendous book *Illusions*, explained it this way: "Every person, all the events of your life are there because you have drawn them there. What you chose to do with them is up to you." Donald certainly believed coincidences have value. Taking it a step further, we suggest that perhaps there are *no real* coincidences—that all events happen to us for a reason. It is merely our job to pay attention to the meaning these incidents have for us as individuals.

In James Redfield's *The Celestine Prophecy*, the main character is told a number of times to pay closer attention to the coincidences that occur in life. This book contains nine key insights for a more enlightened life. The first insight that is revealed centers around life's coincidences. Redfield suggests that a coincidence is a way of drawing us into another mysterious side of life that we already somehow know exists. Such mystery surrounds all of us. We are guided to reflect on the events of our lives and recognize that they go beyond mere chance. There is a deeper, more connected meaning.

CREATING BALANCE

Based on our research (and our own personal experiences), we agree that coincidences have great meaning and impact for all of us. We are all connected by some psychic link of consciousness that draws these events to us. Coincidences are contrived by our subconscious to produce the reality we are supposed to live. This idea holds especially true for twins as they appear to unintentionally create events in their lives to keep a recognizable physical balance between them. See for yourself.

When Walt and John were three years old, John was involved in a car accident where he injured his forehead. The injury was severe enough to require several stitches. A couple of weeks later, while on the way with John to the doctor's office to have his stitches removed, Walt fell against the car door and injured his forehead. Twincidentally, the wound required the same number of stitches as John's.

John and Walt's twincidences did not end in childhood. Walt gave an example: "A few months ago, John and I both strained our calf muscles while running. I have been running for almost twenty years and have never had an injury like this before. But John injured his calf, and shortly thereafter, I injured mine in the same place. What a coincidence! We are used to twin things and this even amazed us."

One of our childhood physical twincidences also occurred when we were about three years old. Nancy was standing near the floor furnace at our grandparents' house. (Yes, the same grandparents as the storm door incident—twin experiences just seemed to follow us there!) The floor furnace was covered with a brown metal mesh grate. Nancy was closer to it than she should have been, but that didn't make the burn hurt any less when she fell and landed on top of that grate.

The result was a burn in the pattern of a checkerboard that extended from the top of her right thigh and ran to her knee. Three days later, Janna was at our aunt's house standing on top of a small gas heater in order to reach the sink in the bathroom. The heater tipped over and fell on top of—you guessed it—her right leg, burning it in exactly the same place as Nancy. Thankfully, this burn was not as extensive as Nancy's, but we'd managed to maintain balance in our lives by each having a burn scar on the back of our right legs.

And then there are Cathy and Chris, who took many years to achieve their physical balance through a twincidence. Cathy retold the two separate incidents, "When we were nearly six years old, my twin released a swing seat that hit me and knocked out my upper left front tooth. In college, I fainted in a bathroom and when Chris found me, she fainted, too. Unbelievably, she hit the floor on the exact same tooth and knocked it out!" We found these twins to be very bonded. They report not only knowing what the other is going to say before words are spoken, but also they have sent each other the same Christmas and birthday cards when they lived in different states.

Small twincidences that do not seem like much add up over the lifetime of twins to have significant impact. Walt and John have lived in different cities and upon reunion have discovered that they each had grown mustaches. Earl and Gearl, more often than not, scored the exact same grade on tests in a variety of subjects. Rhonda and Renee will go shopping and often walk out of the dressing room wearing the same outfit without even knowing the other had selected that outfit to try on. Besse and Esther have had cysts removed from the exact same part of their bodies and have both broken their right wrists at different times.

Whether consciously recognized or not, twincidences are a real part of twins' lives. We think it's important for everyone to pay closer attention to coincidental happenings in life. But we believe this awareness is especially important for twins. The closeness twins share can be magnified as the recognition of twincidence is increased. The hidden meaning behind twincidence enhances the evolution of the twinship and of the individual twins.

Twincidences can also be seen as an extension of the life of sharing for twins. These unexplainable physical and nonphysical events impact the twinergy between twins. Whether they are consciously aware of the effects of these occurrences, we believe twins experience twincidences as a reminder of the special opportunity inherent in living life as twins.

The gift of twinship provides the opportunity to fully appreciate the unique circumstances of a life lived in synchronicity with another person. Attentive observation of twincidences (coincidences for nontwins) brings forth countless lessons that, once accepted and savored, will enrich and strengthen the bond between those who share such experiences.

Twincidence is one way for twins to keep balance in their lives. The real truth is that twins' entire lives are spent on a tight-rope trying to stay in harmony with one another. We have come to think of it in terms of yin and yang.

At age 3 months, no one can tell who is who.

Sharing a good laugh at 18 months.
(Nancy holding the sunglasses.)

Twin dolls about our size when we
were 3 years old (Janna on the right).

Our first visit with Santa was not exactly merry.
(Nancy on the right.)

Looking sweeter than we probably were at 4 years old (Nancy on the left).

In matching outfits fashioned by Mom on our 6th birthday (Janna on left).

1967 Family Portrait
(Nancy on the right)

With Stu on our way to the bottom of the Grand Canyon in 1993 (Nancy on the left).

1998, Big Bear Lake (Nancy on the left).

CHAPTER 7

THE YIN AND YANG OF TWINSHIP

*

The body is healthy only when yin and yang
hold each other in balance.

—Unknown

✳

In 1964 we were only seven years old. And yet we had already established our roles for balance within our twinship. Something we call the yin and yang of twins.

[Nancy—*In our lives, Janna developed her leadership quality within the confines of our twinship very early on. I cultivated acceptance and expectation of her in that role. My young life was made easier by her desire to control our relationship. She kept us organized, while I was content to let her make our decisions. Interestingly, for me, our twin roles were reinforced by society merely through the casting of parts during our second grade theatrical adventures.*

At that time, we were in separate classrooms. Janna's class was performing the play "Cinderella" and my class was performing "Dumbo, the Elephant." She was chosen to play the glamorous Cinderella, while I was given the equivocal leading role of Dumbo.

This selection of roles was perplexing to me in light of our stage experience of the first grade. Janna and I had been little fairy co-stars in a rendition of the "Dance of the Sugar Plum Fairies." We floated on stage in fabulous, identical blue fairy costumes that our mom had made—complete with netting and wings. Our moment was made all the brighter because six little boys swirled behind each of us playing supporting roles for our fairy co-leadership. Now, one short year later, to be thrust into such vastly different parts made me feel less than equal to Janna.

Even Janna's bravest attempts to soothe my pain over these assignments were in vain. Although she astutely pointed out that Prince Charming was neither princely, nor charming, I still saw myself as the goofy kid in the cumbersome gray box. I saw her as the beautiful princess in the lovely dress ruling all that she surveyed.

As has been explained to me on numerous occasions over the years, both Cinderella and Dumbo were the stars of their shows. I'm sure the teachers saw it that way and thought they were setting the stage so that neither of us would have our feelings hurt. However, I couldn't help but feel inferior to Janna. She was playing a beauty, while I played a beast. Her position as twin leader in our lives was cemented for me by that experience.]

The balance that had naturally settled over our twinship in the first few years of our lives was now affirmed by external forces. Janna was cast as the dominant twin and Nancy as the more passive twin. Our twinship yin and yang was born.

YIN AND YANG

As you probably know, ancient Chinese philosophy depicted yin and yang as the dualism of life. These two principles served to explain processes that span and balance opposites, such as masculine and feminine, odd and even, cold and hot, soft and hard, positive and negative, dominant and submissive. Ultimately, yin and yang alternate to produce the whole of beings and things.

Twins are like yin and yang. They achieve balance by cultivating a curious bond of interdependency that allows each of them to play a defined part in their relationship. Division of labor is the normal by-product of this process, as it is with any long-term relationship. Responsibilities are sorted out by the inherent strengths and weaknesses of the players. For example, in a marriage, one person might run the errands, provide meal planning, and do the laundry, while the other one is best suited for paying the bills, handling childcare arrangements, and doing the yardwork. As time goes by, each person settles into his or her specific roles, as is fitting to the particular relationship.

For twins, this role-setting pattern is centered around their synchronized lives from the very beginning. Of course, as children, they don't make any decisions regarding the mundane details of life. However, they still must establish a mechanism for cooperation. Because there are two of them developing at the same time, one naturally steps forward as leader and simply takes charge. The other one readily assumes a less dominant role. Unlike relationships formed in adulthood, there is no judgment about the casting of these positions. This balance, or yin and yang, is necessary for twins' simultaneous co-existence.

WHO'S ON FIRST

How does one twin emerge from the symbiotic twin relationship as the dominant one? How does one become the leader of the twinship?

Several different factors influence this role development in twinships. Dominance in childhood twinship is easy because the decisions revolve around a life of play. It's an innocent organizational tool used to have fun with a constant companion. As twins grow up, the dominant one begins to express an overdeveloped sense of responsibility, and eventually, becomes the caregiver. The nondominant twin relaxes into a mode of being cared for.

Suzanne believed that her twin brother Rich was the most dominant in their twinship—mostly because of his gender. He was sportsminded, which made him competitive in the twinship. However, his outgoing personality was balanced by Suzanne's shyness. She was always comfortable with Rich's dominance in the relationship and enjoyed her role in his shadow.

But dominance in twinship is not predictably gender related. Unlike Suzanne, Vince felt that his twin sister Andrea was the leader of their twinship when they were children. In his timidness, he followed in her footsteps everywhere they went. "Andrea was the 'bossy' twin—she made decisions for us," Vince disclosed. As a result of her outgoingness, Andrea usually made friends for them. These twins, like most twins, carved out roles that worked well for them.

Family Roles

Other forces also play a part in twins settling into their roles. A twinship is really a close relationship existing within a larger relationship—the family. Influences occurring there contribute to defining dominance within the twinship.

Identical twins Walt and John were born first in their family of four children. Despite the fact that these twins were born only five minutes apart, Walt was considered the "oldest" child in the eyes of his family. When the boys would get into trouble, their father would scold Walt severely stating that, as the oldest, he should have known better.

This illogical burden of making the oldest twin the most responsible demonstrates how family pressure can direct one twin toward dominant tendencies.

Walt also held the title of caregiver of these twins. When the two were surveyed at different times, John described Walt as the more responsible one, a caregiver, and the stronger of the two. Walt categorized

John as more demonstrative with his emotions. They both agreed with the other's description. Walt's sense of responsibility put him in the lead to take charge and exercise his dominance. John was content to follow.

These men are comfortable with how they fit into their twinship. The dominance established in their childhood works equally as well for them in adulthood.

This is also true for fraternal twins Sharon and Karen. Sharon was always larger than Karen when they were growing up. This physical difference resulted in Sharon being Karen's protector. With age, Sharon's position expanded to the decision-maker for the twins. "Even our parents helped to solidify my dominant ranking by often looking to me to make decisions for the two of us," Sharon observed.

Karen was and still is quite comfortable following Sharon's lead. Karen candidly characterized Sharon's ability to take control and make decisions as "precise and calculating." Karen feels that Sharon has a knack for weighing everything out, usually making the best choices for them. Although these women are 36 years old with separate lives, Karen lovingly explained that even now, "Sharon tries to protect me from any harm because she wants only the best for me."

Sharon and Karen clearly achieved a balance in their twinship during childhood that did not undergo any pressure to change as they matured. Identical twins Cindy and Wendy, however, switched their childhood roles later in life.

As children, Cindy vigilantly watched over Wendy, guarding her from life's troubles. Cindy was clearly the dominant twin in their relationship. This pattern began in grade school. Though these twins are very close, they are opposites in many ways.

For example, Cindy is right-handed while Wendy is left-handed. Wendy's left-handedness proved to be a bit of a liability during their elementary school days in the early sixties. All left-handers can probably relate to Wendy's frustration at being frequently berated due to the clumsiness associated with being a lefty. Cindy was protective of Wendy's right to be left-handed and once even lost her temper over it, screaming at a teacher who criticized Wendy for cutting a sloppy star.

Cindy and Wendy were separated academically into different class levels, with Cindy attending the more advanced classes. She seemed almost guilty as she related, "This separation held Wendy back and possibly contributed to her disdain for education. I, on the other hand, got a lot out of school and went on to complete a master's degree."

The scales tipped the other way for these twins when Cindy faced challenging health and financial difficulties in adulthood. Wendy came through for Cindy to provide the love and support necessary to help with Cindy's recovery. This role reversal allowed Cindy to let go of her sadness and guilt over Wendy's treatment during their school years. By becoming Cindy's rescuer in adulthood, Wendy gave Cindy a gift of unconditional love that symbolizes the essence of yin and yang in twinships.

The dominant twin gets caught-up in a whirlwind of responsibility and caregiving—taking the lead to protect and nurture his or her twin and the twinship. The nondominant twin plays his or her part. They have freedom within the safety of the twinship to experiment and test boundaries.

During childhood, the dominant and nondominant roles help twins manage their incredible closeness and nurture their relationship. But by the time the raging hormones of adolescence kick in, these roles have been around for many years and can be a source of frustration in the twinship.

If the dominant twin remains too controlling, the twinship can be smothering, especially to the nondominant twin. Too much dominance within the twinship, as with any relationship, can create tension.

Often twins become weary of their type-casting and the nondominant twin tends to rebel as a way to seek balance. It is also a way to begin experimenting with individuality.

Rebel With a Cause

Adolescence brings a questioning of the value of the twinship to each of the twins personally. The inevitable invasion of the outside world into the fortress of the twinship forces every twin to define herself or himself in the nontwin world, not just inside the twinship. As a result, twins begin to develop attitudes about their time together and their time apart.

Quasi-adult, first-time experiences away from one's twin can cause new feelings about oneself to arise. Discomfort with tired, old roles becomes obvious as twins venture outside the twinship. Identical twins Darlene and Arlene are beautiful, redheaded, vivacious women. They captured center-of-attention status as twins. Darlene was the nondominant twin in their twinship. She described her excitement about the discovery of her budding individuality:

"At age 15, while working in a concession stand at a park during the summer, I found out what it was like to be a person without my twin sister. I realized for the first time that I was indeed a totally separate person from her, and I experienced what it actually felt like to be an individual. Our identities had always been tied to being twins.

"In fact, this was such a profound experience for me that I resented her when she stopped by the stand one day to visit with me. It was like she was asserting her dominance and stealing *my* thunder by making us 'the twins' again. This was my first time to know the feeling of receiving attention as an individual, not as a twin."

In our relationship, Nancy felt this urge for independence at age 12.

[Nancy—*I felt an overwhelming need to have control over something in my life. That something turned out to be our family basset hound, Brutus. I spent hours alone in the back yard, teaching Brutus tricks and generally bossing him around. He responded joyously to my attention and we had a great time. This experience gave me a taste for my own authority. I enjoyed this power and took my first steps into a world where I was not a twin following Janna around, but rather an individual in control of myself.*]

Identical twin Gina had a similar awakening. She had always viewed her sister's dominance in their relationship as Tina "running" both of their lives. "Basically, for most of my life, I felt I was always doing things her way and living by her rules," Gina acknowledged. "I felt out of control. As we grew older, I got healthier when I started making my own decisions." She told us that she had to pull away from Tina to gain her sense of herself. Despite the uncomfortable feelings that this change initially evoked in Gina, their twinship needed the balance of each person taking responsibility for herself.

Four People in Two Bodies

During our adolescence, balance outside of our twin-ship was like a rite of passage. We left the sanctuary of our twinship and entered into the turmoil of adolescence. The result was a "split" in our personalities. We became different people outside the twinship than we were inside of it. We were essentially four different people—the two we were with each other in our twinship, and the two others out in the nontwin world. Although submissive inside our twinship, Nancy, surprisingly, was very assertive outside of it. She made many friends who looked to her for the decisions. Her friends were nonjudgmental of her behavior and her spirit began to soar like an eagle.

In the same way, Janna's life outside of our twinship was much different than her dominant role in it. Instead of being the authority figure, she was shy and somewhat intimidated in a big world that did not succumb to her twin-world authority. Therefore, Janna became well-grounded and took a very safe and practical view of life.

Janna played by the rules and rarely risked getting into trouble. Her goal was to be liked and accepted. Nancy, in contrast, continually pushed the edge of the envelope. She never sought acceptance, but rather wanted freedom for herself away from the twinship.

We both became completely opposite people in the "real" world compared to who we were in our twinship.

It was as though the yin and yang within our twinship was offset by the balance we found in our polar existence outside of twinship. In this way, we asserted our identities, yet remained loyal to our twin relationship.

Two People in Two Bodies at Last

We unthinkingly accepted these positions in and out of our twinship until we grew older and wiser. Only then did we come to realize the enormous influence our twin bond had on how we colored the world around us. What seemed so obvious to observers was not as obvious to us because we were living the experience. It took years for us to be able to analyze our own behaviors. Our reality was that together in our twinship, we had developed a full set of traits for one balanced, well-rounded person. A person with leadership skills who could also follow. A person who was sensitive, yet strong. A person who played according to the rules, but wasn't afraid to occasionally color outside of the lines. The trouble was when this "person" went out into the nontwin world, it was really two people who were forced to split apart to tackle life with a woefully incomplete set of tools. Identical twin Josephine summed it up beautifully, "I feel like my sister and I are *one person*, and I feel the most complete and capable when we are together."

Many twins have this feeling of incompleteness without their twin. Janna has often referred to it as feeling like one-half of a person without Nancy. We had to realize that the traits we demonstrated inside our twinship were available to us outside of it and vice versa.

For example, Nancy displayed strength and decision-making capability outside of the twinship, while Janna showed an ability to let go of control and let others take the lead. When we allowed these two sides of ourselves to come into our twinship, we actually integrated them with the roles we had established for ourselves as children. Instead of four personalities, our twinship now has two. Not surprisingly, we are both dominant and passive. Our balance came when we recognized that, in fact, we did have a complete set of tools with which to play the game of life. All of our assets are available for our use, not exclusively inside or outside of the twinship, but in both places.

LESSONS FOR ALL RELATIONSHIPS

If you look at the twin relationship as a microcosm of the yin and yang that we need for all other relationships, you can see that this struggle is not unique to twins. Balance in any relationship can only be attained if each person comes to the table as a complete person—not dependent upon the other person to fulfill their every need. The key is to know who you are and to be that same person inside all of your relationships.

As a singleton, the balance is really only within yourself. As a twin, the process is more complicated because personal balance is intricately intertwined with twin balance. Only when twins are comfortable being the same person inside and outside of their twinship do they bring a complete person into their other relationships.

Much like Sir Isaac Newton's law that for every action there is an equal and opposite reaction, a twinship defines itself in the way the two express traits that fulfill the need for harmony in the twinship. Twins will be able to face the challenges of individual development with greater ease if they give each other the freedom to be who they are, accepting both their similarities and differences inside and outside of twinship.

For growth to occur, any relationship must come under scrutiny and evaluation. This is especially true with a twinship. Know that this is a full-life experience. As aptly epitomized by fraternal twin Vince, "Twins must take a long-term view of their relationship."

Twins are not frozen in time to the place their relationship resides at this moment. Understanding the current status of the twinship leads to opportunity for change and growth. It is critical to remain focused on the inherent specialness of the twinship and not lose sight of that gift, while attempting to achieve balance inside and outside of the twinship.

The first clue of imbalance in the outside world is an awareness of being different when your twin is not with you. Your eyes open even wider when you feel yourself snap back like a rubber band into your old behaviors once you are reunited with your twin. (You will see our discovery and taming of this situation in the next chapter.)

One Picture Is Worth a Thousand Words

The greatest lesson may reside within the very symbol of yin and yang itself. If you look closely at the symbol, you can even visualize the heads of two developing babies positioned, one up and one down, seeking to find comfort and balance in a finite space.

However, the two halves of yin and yang are also enveloped in a perfect infinite circle without a beginning or an ending. As the two halves embrace to fill the circle, each touching its opposite, we see that one half becomes the other. So it is with twins, each half of the pair fully contains the other. The challenge for twins is learning how to see themselves as individuals when they came to this world packaged as a set.

Forming the yin and yang of dominant and passive roles in childhood initially helps twins to define and understand their intimate relationship. As they grow, this balance expands to include how they see themselves outside of their twinship. Ultimate yin and yang balance is achieved when all these roles match. Often this state of balance cannot be attained until twins overcome the dependency of twinship. They must learn how to "separate" from their twinship and those comfortable roles they know so well there. This separation goes well beyond merely being physically apart from one another.

CHAPTER 8

SEPARATE BUT EQUAL

✳

Kari was so painfully shy that I was always uncomfortable being apart from her. I worried about her constantly.

—Shari, 45-year-old fraternal twin

Time away from Shari was refreshing to me. It was a relief to me because the constant comparison of the two of us would stop.

—Kari, Shari's twin sister

Parting is such sweet sorrow . . .

—William Shakespeare

✳

Twins' first separation is often their first day of school. Do you remember your very first day of school? Can you conjure up the smell of those sanitized hallways and well-worn schoolbooks? Do you recall that feeling in the pit of your stomach at the thought of leaving your mommy all day?

For twins that feeling is doubly intense—not only are they away from their mother, but also, they are most often split apart from each other. For the vast majority of twins, this day will be the first day of their entire lives that they spend away from the constant companionship of their twin. This day is terrifying!

In 1963, our parents were told that in order for us to develop fully and make other friends, we would have to be in separate classrooms in the first grade. We had not spent more than a few moments apart in all six years of our lives. Now, suddenly and shockingly, we were separated. And, we did not know why. What had we done to deserve this punishment?

Our fear at being separated from each other during those early weeks of the first grade was indescribable. It was magnified only by our feelings of emptiness and loss. Even though we were surrounded by other children, deep inside, we still felt completely alone because we did not have each other.

You can only imagine the horror for us every day in the lunchroom as we saw each other across the room, but were not allowed to sit together. Since Nancy would not be a "big" girl and stop crying, her teacher had dictated that she should sit alone. We both knew that Nancy was crying because she wanted us to be together.

[Janna—*This scene was like an out-take from the holodeck of "Star Trek, The Next Generation." The computer seemed to freeze the action in the lunch room, except that Nancy and I were still moving. Nancy was crying in what seemed to be slow motion, and I sat in my seat that was several times too big for me, screaming in agony on the inside.*

I was too terrified to cry on the outside, as Nancy was so bravely doing, because I knew that I, too, would be banished to a far-away table. Sitting frozen in the middle of a group of laughing children, feeling alone, was better than actually being alone, like Nancy. Oh, how I wanted to run over to her and take away her pain and humiliation!]

Our mom vividly remembers how once we were home from school, we would cling to each other. "Janna would mumble words of comfort nonstop to Nancy. She would stroke Nancy's hair, hold her hand, follow her everywhere, and say pleadingly, 'It's okay, you probably won't cry at all tomorrow. You will feel much better then. Won't you, Nancy?'"

So begin separation issues for twins. Our first separation was devastating and life-changing. Other twins have expressed similar distress over their first-day-of-school separation:

> " I was very frightened to be away from my sister."
> —Josephine
> "Our first separation in school was bittersweet."
> —Fran, her twin

> "I felt kind of lost, anxious, and fearful when my sister wasn't there."
> —Renee
> "I was sad, isolated, and incomplete without my twin, my best friend."
> —Rhonda, her twin

> "I remember feeling sad that I didn't have my sister there with me."
> —Sharon
> "I had anxiety and was afraid of not having her with me."
> —Karen, her twin

Identical twin Cindy expressed the frustration of most twins over separation when she told us, "Even at a young age, I thought it was stupid for school administrators to think they knew what was best for twins. They didn't know anything about being twins. Why didn't they just ask us?" We have often wondered the same thing.

To Separate or Not

Whether to separate twins as they enter school is a decision faced by all parents of twins. There are those who say that splitting up twins is better because it helps them to become more independent, learn to socialize, recognize themselves as individuals, and develop better communication skills. Others (including us) will tell you that twins need to be left together for as long as possible in order to be given the opportunity to feel safe before being separated. The trauma of starting to school is enough without the added pressure of coping with separation from one's twin.

Of course, separation is inevitable for twins—whether it happens in the first grade or not. But when it happens early in twins' lives, it has a profound effect, not to be underestimated. We believe that, for us personally, our first grade separation had a tremendous impact on the rest of our lives. Janna became excessively dependent on the twinship and developed an oversensitive need to take care of Nancy—complete with constant worry about her health and safety. Nancy, on the other hand, survived that difficult first-grade experience by letting go of the twinship and allowing Janna to carry the responsibility for it.

The Tie That Binds

As we grew up, our twinship did not. When we were together, no matter what our age, we would revert back to our childhood twin selves: Janna as dominant caregiver; Nancy as passive follower. Although those old roles had been our way of maintaining our yin and yang, they were not very effective for our adult lives. We had separated physically (beginning in the first grade), but we were unable to separate psychologically because our first separation had been so traumatic. We were trapped by an underlying fear of losing each other.

What is psychological separation for twins? It's a way of loosening the twin bond without breaking it. It means separating enough from the twinship to feel good about oneself as an individual. Psychological separation is another way for twins to handle the identity crisis that twinship can bring. Balancing the roles of their childhood in and out of the twinship (yin and yang) is only half of the battle. Separating allows twins to release those old roles for more adult ways of dealing with their relationship.

The need to separate psychologically varies among twins. The intensity of this need is not dependent upon whether the twins are living near each other. It is not merely a function of being physically apart and then, like magic, psychological separation automatically follows. Rather, it is paradoxically both an emotional detachment and an acceptance of the twinship. Something clicks for the twins and they realize that they can have their cake and eat it, too. They can have a close relationship and self-identity—at the same time.

Interestingly, we found that the need for psychological separation from one's twin is greater for twins who were abruptly separated in those early school years. Twins who remained in the same classroom, at least for a few years, were much more comfortable with their closeness and twin roles than twins, like us, who were forced to separate before they were ready. Healthy separation seems to come from a soulful acceptance: acceptance of the twinship, of each of the individual twin's identities, and of one's own identity. We think our story will show you the anguish and peace that can come from this acceptance.

The Reunion

We had lived apart for more than sixteen years. However, our desire to live in the same city kept tugging at us. Finally, our dream came true when we were 33 years old.

Our reunion was well-planned and long overdue. It successfully ended our physical separation, but was only the beginning of our psychological separation.

[Janna—*I knew that our impending reunion had a greater meaning. Ironically, I'd told Nancy that I felt we had to live together again to help me let go of my dependency on our twinship. My feeling of being incomplete without her would not be healed until I could understand us as individuals.*

I left Dallas and arrived on Nancy's doorstep in San Diego, California, on January 1, 1991. Despite our immediate elation to be back together, events soon revealed that we had opened a Pandora's box of issues that would challenge us to commit to incredible changes.

Within minutes of entering Nancy's house, I surveyed it and drew conclusions on the rearrangements that would be required to make it "home." My suggestions were seen as criticisms and old wounds for both of us began to bleed resentment and fear.

I had pushed a well-worn button for Nancy. She later told me that childhood memories of my control over her came rushing back. We did not know it then, but Nancy's reaction tipped the scales of balance—forcing us to look for a new yin and yang through psychological separation from our twinship.

If you can call anything a turning point in life, we believe that this was it for us. Nancy, for the first time ever, took an outward, stubborn stand against our usual roles. She attacked me with the viciousness of a lioness protecting her cubs. She shouted, "This is my house! You are a guest! I like it the way it's decorated and you will not be allowed to change anything!" An age-old yell-athon began.

We screamed angry insults at one another, like we had done a thousand other times in our lives. However, deep-down we both knew that this familiar scene was different from all those others. This time the meat of the argument was overtly about control—not about my verbally forcing Nancy to submit to my point of view as she usually did to keep the peace, but rather it was about her finding the su-perhuman vigor to blatantly resist my dominance. She re-soundingly won that battle, leaving us both stunned and confused.

I was horrified and humiliated. I retreated into the room that had been designated as my bedroom (though at that moment I labeled it in my mind as the "guest room") and cried hysterically for hours. I had been in San Diego less than an hour and life as I had always known it seemed to have vanished. Nancy's attempts to reconcile were futile. I refused her advances because this person she had become was a total stranger to me—and our twinship.

Subconsciously, we both knew something was happen-ing to our relationship, though it would take a few years for us to understand and accept it. Nancy had started us on a course of separating from our old roles in the twinship. We

were in the process of giving birth to ourselves as individu-
als. While I was crying and Nancy was pacing, we both be-
gan to doubt the sanity of our decision to live together
again.]

At that time, we had no idea that our reunion
would have such a tremendous influence on our lives.
This move literally turned out to be the motivating
force that caused us to aggressively examine our feelings for one another and our twinship. Living together
helped us to realize that we needed to detach from our
twinship. We could see that we had to release the dependence we had on our childhood roles in order for
our adult relationship to be tolerable.

Same Old Patterns

Slowly, we began to get to know each other as adults.
Being around each other daily enabled old patterns of
interaction to resurface. But those old ways no longer
fit our new selves and our discomfort with each other
grew. It was as if our relationship had been frozen in
time. Once it began to thaw, we discovered that it was
not viable.

Our childhood dependence did not suit our adult
lives. We were no longer those cute little girls who were
the center of attention because they looked exactly
alike. We were adults and had to learn to use adult be-

havior in the relationship that had been engineered and constructed by us during childhood. We had been apart and had each earned graduate degrees, yet when we were together, we immediately reverted to our immature, childhood relationship.

You see, we had spent *so* much time together over the years that we were perpetual children. We continued to react to each other as we had done 24 hours a day for the first six years of our lives, and besides time apart in school, for practically every other moment over the next thirteen years. By the time we were 19 years old, we had logged in more time together than most relationships have over twice that number of years. No wonder we were forever seduced back into our childhood twin roles!

Our Twinship Grows Up (Finally)

Psychological separation from our twinship set us free, at last. We finally opened our eyes to our twinship roles. Unbelievably, until a few years ago, we'd never been able to see our roles, much less label them. Therefore, we didn't know why they weren't working for us.

What for Janna was considered to be loving devotion and sound advice as the caregiving twin, came off to Nancy as criticism and an overbearing need to control her. What Nancy considered to be an honest assertion of her need to be herself, Janna saw as a heartless rejection of her and the twinship. We now understand that these actions, though often misinterpreted by each other, were always motivated by our intense love for one another. We had simply learned a way to express our love in childhood that did not translate as love in adulthood.

We had been physically separated for years, but emotionally, we were still tied to our childhood twin relationship. Whenever we were together, we merely re-enacted our childhood dominant and passive behaviors. The time had come to let go of this aspect of our twinship and find ourselves.

The Dance

We had moments of intense doubt as we maneuvered for position in our evolving relationship. We were whirling around the dance floor, not knowing who was leading and who was following. Because Janna had led for so many years, Nancy's attempts to lead felt awkward and clumsy. Janna was apprehensive when following, and Nancy was uncertain when leading. Yet, we continued to dance.

We focused on the events in the past, then we released them. (Much easier said than done!) We forgave each other for naive transgressions that had driven a wedge in our relationship over the years. We grew to understand that we both can lead. Neither of us has to exclusively follow. This realization goes hand-in-hand with our yin and yang acceptance that we are each a whole, complete person and not one of a packaged set with only one-half of the available traits.

The answers were within us all the time, but we had to increase our awareness in order to finally see how victimized we were by childhood behavior patterns. We're certain that we would not have had the motivation to choreograph the intricate steps of our joyful dance had Janna not moved to San Diego.

Our path to psychological separation was at first glance only a subtle intuition. As we moved through it, we became increasingly aware that it was a necessary part of our relationship. We had to define space for ourselves inside the twinship by letting go of our childhood twin roles. This separation has led to a more fulfilling and less demanding twinship for us.

Together Again

Like us, Vince and Andrea had been separated from each other from kindergarten through high school, causing them much discomfort and confusion. This situation spawned a dependency on their twinship for Vince. Although today they still portray their thirtysomething-year-old twin relationship as very close, they, too, faced their own separation experience which caused them to redefine their childhood closeness.

As with most twins, Vince and Andrea were great friends during high school. They shared the same friends, interests, sense of humor, values, and often, much to Vince's chagrin, his clothes. They even left home together and both enrolled in the University of Kansas to continue their education.

"There was an obvious adjustment that we had to make to no longer living in the same house," Vince remembered. "We really missed each other and for the first time, had to make an effort to see each other." Gone were the days of taking their twinship and time together for granted. As a result, these twins gained a newfound appreciation of each other. They both say that they grew closer over their college days.

After college, Vince succumbed to his wanderlust. He took off on a year of worldwide exploration, leaving Andrea behind. This trip marked their first extended time away from each other. Vince's travels eventually led him to London where he intended to stay for a few months working in an exchange program. But, frankly, he missed Andrea. The best of both worlds seemed possible to him when he and Andrea decided that she could meet him in London for a few months. They planned to live together and share the experience of working in a foreign country. This plan was a miserable failure.

The tiny flat that they were able to rent proved to be a prison for them. Andrea recalled, "The cramped space was just too much togetherness." These twins had gone from being apart to tripping all over each other. "We were at each other's throats," Vince agreed. They both described their living situation as annoying. "Andrea wasn't happy." Vince summarized. "I think we were going in different directions. I was living for the travel experience, day-to-day, trying to unearth and get to know the 'real England.' She felt like she was spinning her wheels in a dud job when she would have rather been with her boyfriend in the States."

As it turns out, Vince feels that this time was the most important point of their relationship. It was the catalyst to help Vince psychologically separate from the twinship. He finally realized that their lives were separate; his plans and dreams were not fulfilling to Andrea. "Our influence over each other diminished a bit over that time, never again to be what it was before. I guess that small feeling of reliance or dependency just died."

Andrea simply believes that they had to be apart for their closeness to remain normal for them. Her view is that "space between us makes for a better friendship."

Time apart created a longing for the twinship for Vince, and a feeling of independence for Andrea. Coming together again helped them see that as adults, they were indeed different from each other. Vince was able to let go of their childhood "ideal" twin relationship and replace it with the "closeness with space" adult twin relationship that Andrea preferred.

Who Am I By Myself?

Growing up means finding yourself. Everyone has a fairly tough time answering the question, "Who am I?" If you are a twin, the question becomes, "Who am I without my twin?" This question is answered through psychological separation. Some twins purposefully attack the challenge of psychological separation head on to help gain their individuality. We unknowingly stumbled into our resolution due to a gnawing need to improve our adult relationship. However, others take a more direct approach. Much like Don Quixote, who tirelessly slashed out at windmills, believing them to be formidable foes, twins often lash out at their twins in an attempt to loosen the bonds that are perceived to tie down their individual identities.

This is why identical twins Chris and Cathy describe being twins as a "tough assignment." Though these women are emotionally very close and are ex-

tremely similar in their tastes, mannerisms, and attitudes, they consciously made the effort to separate psychologically from each other and their twinship in order to achieve their own individuality.

Chris and Cathy were placed in separate classrooms in the first grade through high school. Nonetheless, their twinship remained very close—almost suffo-
cating. They remembered that later in life they actually made an effort to *not* be twins. (How, we wonder,
do you accomplish that mission?)

"The more we saw each other, the more our twinship would rule over our individuality," Cathy recognized. "We intentionally stopped spending time together in college so that we could foster our own identities." Their approach went beyond mere physical
separation and extended into emotional detachment
as well.

These twins understand and appreciate the significance of their relationship as twins. They cherish it as
special, but as Chris explained, "The biological urge to
be close as twins was mixed with emotions to be on our
own and not just one of the twins." As teenagers, they
enjoyed separation because they had freedom and
space in a world and family where they were too often
"treated as a combined entity."

In contrast, Walt and John are good examples of
twins who recognized the need to separate, but who

were quite comfortable with that experience. While these identical twins have a very close relationship, they have managed to remain independent of it. They do, however, admit to making a conscious decision to create individuality for themselves.

John stated that finding his own identity was not necessarily a struggle, but that he simply made a strong effort to establish it. "Ways in which I maintained my own identity from Walt were to wear distinctive clothes, to spend time with different friends, to have separate favorite sports, and to spend time alone away from Walt."

Walt confirmed that they intentionally made space for their own individuality. "We chose different sports to participate in, and therefore, did not compete with each other," he told us. "In this way, we both excelled on our own and received attention and credit as individuals."

We found it interesting that Walt and John were allowed to be in the same classes until the first time they were separated in the sixth grade. We believe that twins who stay together longer have a better sense of their individuality within their twinship. They are a little older and have a better understanding that separation is not abandonment—that it is not forever. The following stories show what can happen when twins are never separated.

In Sync

Besse and Esther were not separated during their school years. Their shared time in the classroom was simply a part of their everyday lives. Never to be questioned. This situation made it easy for them to also study together—compounding their time spent together. They are incredibly comfortable being identical twins and do not seem to have any need for psychological separation. We think this is because they avoided the trauma that comes from being split apart as small children.

Their lives epitomize synchronicity. They both feel that they are very much alike: After more than 80 years, they still look so much alike that people often confuse them for each other; they were married at about the same time to similar men who both accepted their twinship without jealousy; they both express that their twinship has been a wonderful blessing; and they both say that they are like one person.

These twins even dressed alike until Besse married and they were actually separated *for the first time in their lives!* This separation was not easy for them. Besse pointed out the issue that being apart created for them: "During the time I lived far away from Esther, we were both never completely happy—except when we visited each other."

These ladies are now living single lives, as both of their husbands have died. This has made them even closer than before. (Hard to imagine!) Besse and Esther have never really been forced to accept or adjust to separation in a way that most twins do. They did not have to learn to be apart in school, to make other friends, or to discover themselves without the other. They simply nestled down into their twinship like a soft, old sweater—comfortably allowing it to be the driving force of their happy lives.

As amazing as Besse and Esther's twinship is, we found that the most astounding example of twin tolerance has to be the twin pair of Earl and Gearl. Like Besse and Esther, Earl and Gearl were never separated during their school days, having all their classes together through high school.

These twins have a remarkable acceptance of themselves as twins. In fact, Earl and Gearl were the only twins who responded to our survey who indicated that neither of them was dominant, nor a clear caregiver in their twinship. Their synchronicity is exemplified by their wondrous lives. Earl and Gearl hold the same degree in Business Administration. Their strong religious preferences resulted in both of them becoming ministers. They were stationed in Tacoma, Washington, together while in the Navy and were the best man at each other's weddings, both in 1955. They both enjoy

singing and golfing. The profound unity of their twinship inspires awe, even in us. They have a comfortable
balance in their twinship. They are living parallel
lives—in perfect yin and yang.

The fact that they didn't have to struggle with separation issues early in their lives helped them to gain a
contentedness with their roles as twins. This way identity issues never really surfaced for them. They never
faced the world for any extended period of time without each other and their twinship. Clearly, Besse and
Esther and Earl and Gearl have managed to escape the
separation anxiety, in the classic sense, that we found
most twins must face during their adult lives.

As the Pendulum Swings

While the separation issue is certainly unique to each
twin pair, remarkably the extent of frustration with inevitable psychological separation appears to be linked
to how well physical separation was handled in early
childhood.

Obviously as small children, twins cannot compre-
hend the issues involved in separation of themselves
from the twinship into the two individuals who they
truly are. Thoughtful approaches to that first physical
separation of twins by parents and school officials is essential. As evidenced by our separation story, the con-

sequences of a premature school separation experience can have a significant impact on the dynamics of the twinship when the time comes for a psychological parting.

Later in twins' lives, separation from the twinship in order to cultivate an identity for each twin is a necessary component to the growth of the twinship. Our "separation" absolutely did not mean a parting of the ways. In fact, it has brought us closer together. It means being together as whole persons who love and cherish the twin relationship, but without the loss (or denial) of our individual selves.

It all seems to boil down to self-love. We believe that many of the woes of the planet could be cured if we all accepted our abundance of self-love. But for twins, it is often hard to love oneself as an individual because the individual identities get so tied to the twinship. The love of the twinship can consume the love of the self. However, it's essential for twins to learn self-love in order for them to comfortably face the nontwin world with confidence—as a singleton.

Psychological separation is the bridge that closes the gap between the twinship and the individual selves. It allows the twins to be who they are, not merely defined as a twin. It is like a marriage. That union is much healthier and happier if both participants are self-confident, complete individuals—not waiting for the other one to fill them up. No one can be everything to someone else, not even a twin.

Our lives and our twinship have consisted of a series of pendulum swings. We had to experience the full extreme of being completely dependent upon one another in childhood to the other extreme of being apart and feeling confused for many years before we could find a comfortable spot in the middle.

This slow swinging of extremes over our lifetime has guided us to a better relationship. Psychological separation from the twinship has allowed the pendulum to stop in the center.

Nancy had to feel Janna's pain in order to realize the challenge Janna faced in separating from the pattern of responsibility. Janna had to feel Nancy's frustration in order to appreciate the obstacles Nancy faced in gaining control over her own life. Janna had to separate from the twinship without fear and Nancy had to return to it without resentment.

These challenges resulted in a few years of discomfort with our twinship that left us each longing for reconciliation. Fortunately, we took the time to identify the root of the issue—that we needed to establish an adult twinship which had space for us as "the twins" and as individuals.

Sadly, in some twinships, an unmet need to psychologically separate can form a canyon between the twins which can seem too large to traverse. The result is a tragic, literal and figurative, breaking of the twin bond.

CHAPTER 9

WHEN THE BOND BREAKS

✴

Being a twin is a curse, because you struggle to be an individual, but everyone else sees you as a reflection of someone else. You are constantly being compared to your twin ...The competition creates great resentment.

—Arlene, 48-year-old identical twin

It can be a curse if one twin is so dependent on the other one and never learns to be self-sufficient. I know sisters who are two to three years apart and are closer than my twin and me.

—Darlene, Arlene's twin

If you bring forth what is within you,
what you bring forth will save you.
If you do not bring forth what is within you,
what you do not bring forth will destroy you.

—Jesus of Nazareth

The headline read: "TWIN ORDERED TRIED IN PLOT." Jeen and Sunny Han are beautiful, 22-year-old, Asian identical twins who were co-valedictorians of their high school graduating class. How could these two women of such tremendous potential end up with their lives exposed on the pages of the L.A. Times?

Unbelievably, in early 1997, Jeen Han and two teenage boys were arrested and accused of conspiracy to murder Sunny. Police suspect Jeen wanted to assume Sunny's identity and that she feared Sunny was going to kill her if she didn't kill Sunny first.

The reasons for destruction of this twinship may never be wholly known. Jeen has not told her story yet. Sunny has. Even in the face of obvious betrayal, Sunny remained loyal to her sister and the twin bond. She adamantly defended Jeen outside of the courthouse on the day of the arraignment. Sunny felt that Jeen was an innocent victim of manipulation by the two boys. She refused to believe that Jeen would have tried to kill her due to jealousy, exclaiming, "If anyone is jealous, it is me, as Jeen was always smarter and more artistic than me." Sunny insisted that the two are best friends who tell each other everything.

Their story is complex and unresolved, yet it opens our eyes to the tragic problems that can develop within twinships. What seems to be so magical to the outside world can evolve into a breeding ground for jealousy, fear, and greed, thus leading to a severance of that special gift of the twin bond.

While the causes of the problems in this twinship remain a mystery, a closer look at the tension that builds in twinships can help us see how the pressures of being a twin may have contributed to Jeen and Sunny's predicament.

TWIN CONFLICT RESOLUTION NEEDED HERE

Of all of life's certainties, one stands out above the rest: any time we venture into relationships with other humans, conflict is inevitable. The degree of conflict can range from a mild misunderstanding to an irreparable chasm. The more time we spend with any one person, the greater the probability we will encounter confrontation.

If you have siblings, you know the inherent rivalry in those relationships. Life with a sibling invariably involves a battle or two over some unresolved territory. For the most part, we all grow up and learn the necessary communication skills to mend childhood disputes and allow lasting adult relationships to form. In fact, for many people some of the closest relationships they will ever know in their lives are with family members.

Twins are no exception to this rule. Their time spent together is practically endless. By now you have a sense of the strength of the glue that cements many twins into an intimate relationship that cannot be matched by any other human experience. However, as with Sunny and Jeen, some twinships absolutely cannot endure the pressures of this extreme interaction on the human playing field.

Trouble within twinships can result in a long, slow erosion of the twin bond that has a far-reaching impact on the health of the twinship. Often problems begin from simple issues. One such factor that can chip away at the twin bond is the bringing of a significant other into the twinship.

A Difficult Choice

For the most part, we all want to find a mate. The urge that pulls us toward a lover is very strong. However, it can be quite challenging when the budding romance involves a twin. An eternal triangle is formed that needs some special nurturing. Sometimes significant others inadvertently drive a wedge into the twinship which fractures the twin bond to such an extent that destruction of the twinship is the only way to release the pressure valve.

Such was the case with Vivian and Helen. These

fraternal twins grew up in San Antonio, Texas, in the early 1900s. As children, they were inseparable and shared the same classroom from grade school through high school. They moved to Austin together to attend the University of Texas (UT). They lived in tandem, until the fateful day when Helen fell in love. "When Helen married, she and I parted and grew further and further apart," Vivian recalled. What really happened to this twinship? It's not as simple as Helen marrying to push Vivian away.

The struggle for balance in their twinship was a long, rocky road. When asked which was the most dominant, each felt that the other was the dominant twin. Not surprisingly, this revelation was not free from resentful innuendo.

When describing her sister, Helen insisted, "Vivian feels that she knows more than I do in most ways. She would like to be the caregiver, but she is very annoying to me and is not successful." Vivian, with similar indignation, reported, "Helen wanted and tried to be the dominant one." These two women could not find comfortable roles for themselves in their twinship.

As a result of their conflicts, Vivian felt stymied by the twinship. "Our parents insisted that we dress alike and act alike. I found those ideas to be so old-fashioned." Vivian struggled to be her own person, and after their graduation from UT, she began traveling far and wide, becoming a great adventurer. This was a remarkable pursuit for a woman in the 1920s. Her journeys ended in New York City where she attended graduate school. She found herself becoming more independent as she searched for a life of her own. In reality, she was running away from the twinship, instead of confronting the problems she had with Helen.

Meanwhile back at home, Helen was leading a less exciting, but equally fulfilling life by falling in love with her college sweetheart. "Vivian was jealous of my marriage because I was happy," Helen claimed. "She never achieved that in her life." Helen sadly noted that Vivian never got close to Helen's husband, although Helen believed that he would have done anything for Vivian. "He was a wonderful person, very loving to our parents (like a son), but that, too, got Vivian upset."

For her part, Vivian snarled, "Her husband was a very stupid man. I could never be around him for that reason." She showed further disdain for Helen's husband by adding, "She unhooked the umbilical cord from my mother and hooked it into him. She wanted everyone to kowtow to him and his wishes—I never would."

Even though Helen's husband died in 1989, the bitterness still simmered in their twinship. They couldn't break through that wall of resentment that had been standing for over fifty years. These twins were 89 years old when they independently filled out our survey. Each response was laced with anger.

Yet beneath all the hateful words, Vivian and Helen hinted at a secret longing for their twinship. Vivian told us, "We do not agree on anything, but still feel responsible one for the other." And Helen confessed that they called each other every day—usually twice a day.

These women had a powerful twinship that was crippled by the choices they made—one choosing to venture around the world and study in hopes of diminishing the hold the twinship had on her, while the other one chose a more settled life in a marriage. Vivian needed to escape from Helen's critical involvement in her life. This drastic departure from Helen's life drove Helen to seek companionship in her husband. They each seemed to be looking outside their twinship for the wholeness that they could have found within it.

In the fall of 1996, shortly after their 91st birthday, Helen died after many years of being home-bound. Ironically, Vivian, who was in much better health and regularly attended the theater and symphony, died within three short months of her sister. We will never know whether Vivian and Helen actually healed the deep wound in their twinship before they left the earth, but the twincidental nature of their deaths gives us hope that they are working out their problems in another realm.

A Hope for More

While Vivian and Helen did not understand the significant impact of Helen bringing a husband into their twinship, Fran and Josephine clearly know that Josephine's husband is a major reason for the discord in their twinship.

Fran would like nothing more than for Josephine and her to be best friends. Unfortunately, according to Fran, Josephine's husband "does not understand a twin relationship." The resentment Fran feels for Josephine's husband began with their wedding. As this marriage was Josephine's second, the couple chose to have a quick wedding and would not wait for Fran to come from the east coast to be a part of their California ceremony. Fran still hurts from Josephine and her husband's hurried decision.

Interestingly, Josephine *concurs* with Fran's perception of Josephine's husband. Josephine told us that he's self-centered and lacks a family orientation. She said he's very jealous of family members and wants to move Josephine further away from Fran, now that they are both living on the west coast.

Although Josephine's marriage is a barrier to her bond with Fran, other turmoil haunts this twinship. Fran has a long history of disapproval of Josephine's friends and lifestyle. She harbors a fear that Josephine will do something to embarrass her when they are together.

As critical as Fran's description of Josephine is, an underlying yearning to have a closer relationship with Josephine can be detected in her responses to our questions. She misses having Josephine in her life and wants reconciliation.

Josephine is less aware of how displeased Fran is with her in their relationship, but she vividly sees the issue with her husband. She writes, "I would love to move closer to Fran, even if the price is my marriage." Though these twins live in the same state, the roughly one hundred miles between them appear to be too vast a distance for them to cross. We think that they merely need to take that first step.

Evaluating Fran and Josephine's surveys gave us considerable hope in the healing power of twinship. Both are magnetically drawn to each other. They both indicated that the greatest obstacle for peace in their twinship is Josephine's husband. Fran is confident that she could positively impact Josephine's life if given the opportunity to see her more often. Josephine believes that the key to her happiness lies in reuniting with

Fran. What this twinship needs is a giant dose of honest togetherness, for the love between them could not be any stronger.

TWIN VS. TWIN

Making a choice between a love relationship and one's twin is really an impossible decision. Fran and Josephine exemplify the negative consequences that can occur when a twin feels he or she is in competition with a significant other for the attention of his or her twin. The opposite, yet equally difficult, situation is when the twins themselves are jealous of one another.

I Saw Him First

We are lucky, as we always had different taste in boys and men. Though we were critical of each other's choices, causing issues of another sort, we never had the experience of competing for the affections of the same person. Gina and her identical sister Tina were not so lucky.

These twins have shared just about everything for most of their lives. Growing up in a rural area served to solidify their bond, as they were some distance from other friends. Their love of horses also brought them closer together. Things were fine until they became old enough to date.

For some reason, Tina would sabotage Gina's relationships. On one occasion she even stole a boyfriend from Gina and pretended not to understand why Gina was so upset by it. At other times, upon first meeting Gina's boyfriends, Tina would "warn" them about Gina's tendency to "abuse guys." Needless to say, these activities had a detrimental effect on their twinship.

A recurring theme in this twinship is that of competition and jealousy. In contrast to seeing their relationship as a partnership, this twin pair seems to view their twinship as a contest. From sports to grades to catching a man, they were continually focused upon "one-upping" each other. Perhaps Tina's motivation for scaring men away from Gina was to be the victor in the love wars, thereby beating Gina time and again.

This twinship still hasn't recovered from all the resentful incidents that have taken place. Gina misses Tina in her life terribly but feels, "Tina never misses me." The inability to effectively communicate about their twinship has resulted in a deep sense of loss in their lives. This void can only be filled by a sincere effort to mend the twin bond because, as we saw with Vivian and Helen, it's a force that will not simply go away if ignored—that ghost of your twin will somehow haunt you despite your rejection of it.

Of course, the entry of a significant other into a

twinship isn't always a recipe for disaster. A mindful introduction of a significant other into a twinship can be quite successful, even though an occasional storm should be expected. For instance, Suzanne's husband is usually very tolerant and supportive of her twin Rich. But when conflicts arise, Suzanne thinks it may be due to her husband being jealous of Rich. She suggested, "Perhaps he is really jealous of my *relationship* with Rich, not of Rich himself." This profound insight hits home for twinships. No one can have the same relationship with a twin that their twin does. This isn't always an easy pill for others to swallow.

THE FACES OF RESENTMENT

Twins grow up and learn to interact with the world outside the comfort zone of the twinship. However, they go through phases and mood swings about being twins. Life as twins brings on unique struggles for individuality and sometimes resentment of the twin experience.

Sharing Pangs

One aspect of twinship that can plant seeds of resentment is the sharing experience. Although many twins aren't bothered by this occurrence and accept it as the status quo, some twins felt like they were denied the right to have something all to themselves. That two of the same gifts were given, or one gift had to be shared, took the specialness out of the gift.

On occasion, Janet and Graham were told that they couldn't have something they wanted because there were two of them. The implication was if there were only one, then that one would have gotten the coveted object. Janet also felt some animosity over sharing her birthday with Graham. As a child growing up, she felt that there was no escape from the situation. "You have a shared birthday and party. It's never just *your* day."

The most bitter example of this type of resentment was revealed by identical twin Darlene. When we told her what a blessing being twins was for us, she asked, "Why would being a twin be a blessing? It placed a financial burden on my parents because every toy, article of clothing, and school expense had to be paid twice. I had to do without a lot because of the expense involved."

While growing up, Darlene must have heard that twins caused a bad financial situation in their home. It's sad that any parents would give their children the unnecessary guilt of adult financial problems. Even greater sadness fills our hearts that the precious gift of twinship was somehow lost on these twins.

Darlene's twin, Arlene, bluntly exclaimed, "It has not been my experience that being a twin is a gift. It is a happenstance of life which one has to make the best of. In fact, it presents more problems and challenges than the average person has to deal with during his/her life." Obviously, Darlene and Arlene have not been able to make peace with their twinship.

Resentment runs deep for them, and not just as a consequence of sharing. Arlene was even resentful of having to dress like Darlene. Dependency in the twinship was a burden that neither twin wanted to carry. They each felt strongly about gaining independence from one another. Arlene, who is the dominant twin, reflected on the time when Darlene developed her independence and said, "She *lived* to preserve that independence. It has never been resolved." Arlene and Darlene's quotes at the beginning of this chapter signify their discomfort with the dependency inherent in a twinship. Interestingly, they were the only twins we surveyed who portrayed twinship as a curse.

OUT OF THE DARKNESS

These stories show a dark side of twinship that you have probably never contemplated before. Twinship is not a Zen state of blissful existence that allows two special children to go through life somehow spared the tri-

als and tribulations of singletons. The twin relationship is wonderful, but it can be overwhelming. We appreciate the difficulties faced by twins who struggle
with their closeness. We, too, had our dark side.

Our Rift

As hard as it is, even for us, to believe, we had a time in
our lives when for about two years we barely spoke to
one another. We were 18 years old, in our second year
of college, and living together in a small, two-bedroom
duplex.

You must know that we had not done a very good
job up to this point of setting any boundaries between
us. In "Twinspeak," we explained how quickly we forgave each other after an argument—almost instantane-
ously. It seemed we took the easy road to resolve our
conflicts in order to keep harmony in our relationship.
Because we didn't know how to have individual personal space, we started getting on each other's nerves.

Nancy began to pull away from the twinship. That
taste of independence she savored in the backyard
with Brutus grew into a desire to be away from Janna's
control.

Our arguments became more and more heated. We
eventually lost the ability to rapidly get over the result-
ing wounds. Instead, we both closed down and stop-

ped speaking to each other. This behavior would last for days. Our only communication would be the dirty looks that passed between us in the hallway.

As a definitive assertion of her independence, Nancy suddenly moved out.

[Janna—*I could not have been more shocked. We were in the middle of one of our fights. Nancy's first words to me in days were, "I've rented my own place. I move in two weeks." I felt like a flaming knife had just been stabbed into my heart. The saddest part was that I could see pain in Nancy's eyes, too.*]

At that time, we simply did not have the skills to let go of the dependency of our relationship. Unable to identify and resolve our closeness issues, we turned from each other. Nancy could no longer accept Janna's dominant role and Janna could not give it up. Janna could no longer tolerate Nancy's indifference, but Nancy was not able to learn responsibility inside our twinship.

After Nancy moved out, our friendship waned. We no longer sought out each other's company, and eventually, did not see each other at all. About one year into our separation, Nancy continued her search for herself by moving 300 miles away to attend Baylor Medical Technology School in Dallas, Texas. *That* separation proved to be too much for us to bear.

Though our twin bond had bent, it was far from

broken. So, the silence of the previous year or so was smashed as those miles apart helped us to see how much we truly missed each other. It was easier to stay mad at each other when we knew the other was only a few blocks away. Hundreds of miles was just too *real* of a separation!

We know now that our problem was that we were too dependent on our twinship. This situation was a combination of our childhood roles not growing up with us and a need to psychologically separate. Unfortunately, as you know, we didn't address the issue until our San Diego reunion, fifteen years later. However, we are extremely thankful to have done so—no matter how long it took. It required facing the dependency and co-dependency of our twinship.

TWINS AND CO-DEPENDENCY

In any relationship, too much dependency on one person is a formula for disaster. This behavior is commonly defined in contemporary terms as co-dependency. Twinship could actually be the poster child for co-dependency. No other situation in human experience involves so much interaction over such a prolonged period of time. Twins' interdependence can easily become a form of dependence.

The use of the word "co-dependency" was first

coined in the late seventies as a way to define persons whose lives were strongly affected by someone with chemical addictions. Today, the definition has broadened beyond that. Simply stated, a co-dependent is a partner in dependency.

Typical co-dependent behavior looks like this: A co-dependent person is an obsessive "helper." This need to help others turns the co-dependent into a caregiver who has a strong tendency to be controlling. Everyone knows a well-meaning friend, relative, or acquaintance who takes on the world's problems to the sacrifice of their own needs. They "worry themselves sick" about other people. Bending over backward to take care of others results in the co-dependent often feeling that no one is ever *really* there for them.

As a result of this behavior, the person being "taken care of and worried about" also becomes a co-dependent—that is, they start to rely on the other person to meet their needs, thus enabling the caregiver's actions. The vicious cycle begins, as co-dependents continue to reinforce these behaviors in each other.

In a twinship, this pattern is usually positive and necessary for childhood interactions. It's a response to so much time spent together. Again, the dominant and passive roles produce organization in an intense relationship that would otherwise be fairly chaotic. Co-dependency of twins only turns into a problem if twins do not learn to handle their conflicts and their relationship in a more adult manner.

Is It a Fit?

Our dark side was certainly a teaching model for co-dependency. Janna tended to over-care and Nancy wanted that. We fed into each other, keeping the madness alive. Though we didn't know what we were doing, we rejected our co-dependency by running away from our twinship.

It doesn't take a huge leap of faith to also fit the other twins from this chapter into the definition of co-dependency. For example, the pressures of Helen's dominance and control drove Vivian from the security of her twinship. Vivian's attempts to release herself from Helen backfired into a lifelong tug-of-war on their hearts and a quasi-addiction to feuding over their differences.

Fran demonstrated some classic control signs in her twinship with Josephine. Her belief that she had to excel to somehow make up for Josephine's inadequacies speaks volumes about her need and quest for approval. She also felt embarrassment for her sister and wished her to be different. Fran could benefit from the conclusion we finally came to: you can't change your twin into the person that you would like them to be. (Just as we can't change anyone on this planet, with the notable exception of ourselves.) Psychologist Dr. Wayne W. Dyer described it perfectly when he said in *Your Erroneous Zones*, "Love is the ability and willingness to allow those that you care for to be what they choose for themselves, without any insistence that they satisfy you."

Darlene and Arlene's deep-rooted resentment of their twinship has had remarkably negative effects on their ability to even enjoy each other as sisters, much less twins. Their twin bond has been shattered, and neither woman seems to want to salvage what remains. They have chosen to live life as singletons and deny the specialness of their circumstances.

You can see how twins struggle to know where the twinship ends and the self begins. Some twins can't handle the strain of maintaining the twinship, especially at the carefree level of childhood, while trying to find comfort with themselves as whole human beings or with other people.

Every human has a dark or shadow side—that place where we store the parts of ourselves that we don't love, the parts that have felt rejection and pain. We must turn the light on those darkened corners if we are to reach wholeness as individuals. Those repressed portions must be integrated into our beings. Carl Jung pointed out the danger of not illuminating the dark side when he advised, "What we choose to ignore ends up controlling our lives." A damp, cold basement left to its own devices will grow unwanted mushrooms and mold. Those unexamined, uncomfortable parts within us (and our twinships) will continue to ulcerate, unless properly tended.

EQUAL PARTNERING

As true as this is for each person, it is equally true for relationships. The mere history intrinsic in the relationship called twinship results in many years of built-up issues. Twinships have a large warehouse of stored boxes that are filled with unpleasant experiences that somehow managed to damage the twinship. Happy experiences don't get stored there, only the stuff that prevents healing. We know that we had suppressed numerous uncomfortable instances, instead of facing them. That dreaded quick-to-fight-quick-to-make-up philosophy that we generated on the kitchen floor as toddlers gave us permission to pack away negative feelings and deny any rough edges to our twinship. We, too, bought into the illusion that twinship was somehow blessed and immune to dark times. (Or at least our denial of those times kept them away from our focus.)

Denial is another one of the defining characteristics

of co-dependency and twinships are chock-full of it. Vivian focused her anger about her relationship with Helen on Helen's husband, instead of acknowledging that the real problems were in the twinship. Fran and Josephine are quick to blame Josephine's husband for the rift in their twinship, yet ultimately, it's the choices they've made over their 61-year twinship and the reasons they made them that have created their situation. What was the role of Fran's perpetual judgment of Josephine in some of Josephine's "bad" choices? Darlene and Arlene have chosen to deny their twinship altogether, as that's the only way they can escape the pain within it.

Twinship is indeed a partnership. At times that partnership is a co-dependent one emerging as a mechanism to endure the scrutiny of being twin children. We have shown how successful our co-dependency was during our childhood. We were extremely happy children and our twinship wrapped us in a joyful glow that made us feel remarkably complete—content with one another's company. We really didn't need much else to occupy us. For all practical purposes, we were in complete balance with our roles in our twinship.

Then the inescapable occurred—we grew up. As simple as that sounds, it took us a long time to figure out where our precious childhood twinship fit into our complex adult lives. Other twins face this dilemma also, moving through their relationship like "Big Time Wrestlers" circling one another, trying to find the perfect position in a competition between the love of the twinship and the desire to know life without it. This wrestling match is part of growing up as a twin.

The match can be brutal, with the twinship coming out the loser as we saw with Vivian and Helen, and as it appears with Darlene and Arlene. The match can also run its course with the twinship ultimately winning the battle, as in our case.

Our advice to twins is to stop the madness, get out the big spotlight, and shine the light into that warehouse of boxes and open them up. Become aware of those old wounds that have been covered over. You must talk about the twinship. Have an honest discussion of the feelings you had when you realized you'd outgrown the childhood concept of your twinship. We've spent many hours evaluating those dark corners, bringing out the parts we had rejected over the years. Our feelings spanned from deep pain to pure elation. We discovered that we were both carrying around misplaced guilt and anger from the past.

A great lesson can be learned from Vivian and Helen. Driving a stake in the heart of a twinship can only leave holes in the souls of the twins. Darkness cannot be avoided in this life. The challenge is how we bring the darkness to light for change and growth. This advice is not only for twins. Accept and embrace those times of conflict and turmoil, for at the core of each is a lesson. Find the lesson in those experiences and then release them. We can be lighter, more fulfilled human beings. A treasure chest of knowledge is hidden away within each of us. We truly can attempt to reach wholeness when we do as Jesus recommends: bring forth what is within you (and your twinship).

CHAPTER 10

THE EARTH
AND THE SKY

✳

As I recall the wonder of your lives, I see you now as you were from the beginning—each one complete as an individual, yet somehow more complete together. Your different personalities dovetail with each other to delight and charm those you encounter on your paths. You have exceeded every dream and expectation I had for you by always having grander dreams and expectations of your own. To be inspired by your children, as I am, surely is every parent's greatest desire.

—Jo, Nancy and Janna's mother

An unexamined life is not worth living.

—Socrates

✳

Fran Dancing Feather announced matter-of-factly: "Nancy, you are Eagle Woman. You are of the sky. You know freedom and your spirit soars. Independence is your nature. Janna, you are Buffalo Woman. You are of the earth. You are a great provider, not only for family but for community. Responsibility is your purpose.

"But the Wolf watches over both of you. Together, you are the Wolf. He is a cunning, free-spirited predator like the Eagle, yet he is loyal and grounded in family like the Buffalo. Wolf is the great teacher."

This chapter is about our evolution as individuals and as twins. We have approached it in what we believe to be an objective manner. It is the only chapter that we have literally written together at the same time.

LESSONS IN SHARING

All their lives, Nancy and Janna shared everything. A hamburger was cut exactly in half and split between them. A Coke was poured equally into two glasses. They colored in the same coloring book. A warm bath was drawn for them to share. What appeared to be half to others was always enough for them as twins.

Sharing is one of the earliest teachings in childhood. Parents struggle to avoid having their child labeled as selfish. Thus, they expend a great deal of effort explaining why toys should be shared with others. Some nebulous reward was to be earned through giving something up for someone else. Ah, but sharing was different for twins. To Nancy and Janna, it was the status quo for as far back as they can remember. As children, they shared time in the high chair, a double stroller, side-by-side doctor visits, and even a tonsillectomy for two.

It was not about having anything taken away, but rather sharing was about having someone else there to enjoy and enhance the moment. Everyone knows that many pleasures are amplified and many unpleasant experiences are more bearable in the presence of another. Twins have the reality of another's presence as a constant in their lives. The notion of not sharing throughout the day was as unthinkable as the thought of being alone in the world.

This life of sharing taught the lessons of compassion, unselfishness, courtesy, and anticipation. The process was simple and efficient, yet profound in its meaning. It brought them closer to each other and awakened them to the specialness of their relationship. Once awake, twins can more easily tap into their power. A power that grows through living life in a world of sharing—the power of more.

TWO MEANS MORE

Double your pleasure, double your fun! Two by two! Double coupons! Twice as nice! Two for the price of one! Our lives are filled with expressions telling us that more is better. Twins are the essence of "more."

Janna and Nancy have more fun together than apart. They get more joy from simple moments, more wonder. More lessons are brought forth for the learning, as each one's lessons contribute to the development of both. More meaning is captured through each experience because more information is processed by the two of them.

They can do more. They can serve more. Think about the combined power of twins. They can get more attention side-by-side. In that way, more messages are delivered. They can help each other seek the power within each individually and know that together the power is magnified.

The Power of Two

Twins are not an accident. The power that created them is omnipotent. Although the fact that two beings are created at the same time seems to be a genetic mishap—occurring for no apparent reason—it has a purpose. Each one of us has a purpose, but twins are blessed with also having a dual life purpose. Let's face it, if it didn't have unique meaning, everyone would be a twin.

The significance is in being right here, right now with someone who is *exactly* the same age as you. Probably someone you chose to be here with. Therefore, inherent in the twinship is a source of that same power that brought twins into existence in the first place.

When Janna and Nancy discuss this power, they acknowledge it as a universal power supply that energizes everything they do. This force is not unique to them, but is available to everyone. They just have a head start because their shared life has connected them in such a way that their receipt of universal energy is efficient. This advantage was only fully realized when their awareness of the power increased.

This power is often manifested for twins when their two heads, in fact, prove to be better than one. This happens frequently for twins. Nancy and Janna recognize it by the people they draw into their lives when they are together. They have noticed that they seem to meet the right people, at the right time. Teachers appear when Janna and Nancy are ready to be students. A literary agent came into their lives and ended up changing the focus of this book. Editors appeared to help them develop the writers within. A young adventurer passed through to provide guidance on ascending Mt. Kilimanjaro. An intuitive economist taught them the wisdom to be heard in silence.

Events such as these can come and go, often getting lost in the noise of everyday life. The challenge is to pay attention and contemplate such seemingly chance encounters. Nancy and Janna intentionally cultivated their awareness capabilities by keeping track of these fortuitous occurrences through diaries and gratitude journals. Patterns were revealed before their very eyes. They discovered that serendipity often showcases signposts on the roadway of life. Now, twincidences have more meaning to them than ever before.

THE ULTIMATE RELATIONSHIP

In this life, we cross paths with many people, some remaining with us for years, others not. All encounters have some meaning for us. However, having a twin is beyond a chance meeting. It is a relationship that begins before birth.

If you imagine having another person's life in perfect synchronicity with your own, you can appreciate the opportunity having a twin affords. It has the potential of being the longest-lasting relationship of your life and is something more than any other sibling or parental relationship. Simultaneous development allows twins to enter into and conquer all stages of life with someone who is the same age. With others, the age difference is ever-present, setting those relationships apart from twinships.

The novel circumstances surrounding twins' lives give them an appreciation and empathy for one another that really cannot be matched with anyone else. Here is a person in your life who knows you so intimately that it is hard to fully distinguish your thoughts and feelings from theirs. The result is a relationship of trust, sharing, challenge, and fulfillment. Nancy and Janna say it is the ultimate relationship.

They see twinship as a dress rehearsal for life. The lessons that are presented in this ultimate relationship are gifts to bring to the world. Endless possibilities exist for simple teachings such as: be considerate of others; hold hands often; share what you have; spend time with those you love; have many hugs every day; keep cramped quarters neat; compromise is always possible; be honest with each other; work on problems as they arise; keep a secret if you are told one; clean out useless garbage regularly; listen carefully; let others be what they want to be; and, cherish each other.

The key to success in using these lessons taught by a twinship is in applying them consciously every day. To do this, take a step away from yourself (and your relationship, be it a twinship or otherwise) and simply be an objective witness of your own behavior. Are you reacting in the way that you want to? Are you giving your power away to someone else? Are you really listening to the other person, letting them fill you up with their words before you speak? Are you responding honestly? (Even to these questions!?) If you are satisfied with your answers, then you have just increased your awareness of yourself. That means you are working on yourself, not on the other person. A better you makes for a better partner in any relationship or twinship.

Can We Keep It Simple?

As simple as these teachings appear on the surface, they are far from easy. For twins, one of the obstacles in learning these lessons occurs when one twin tries to separate from the other twin. The bond keeping the two together is powerful. To get away from it, and then to be comfortable as an individual, is truly a test. The inadvertent psychological hold that twins have on one another can be counterproductive to individual growth and development. Thus, the childhood lessons given by the gift of twinship are often buried under fear—fear of being alone coupled with fear of not being alone.

One twin's desire to carve out a special place alone

is not intuitive within the twinship. The process can be misconstrued as rejection, even betrayal by the other twin. Nancy experienced these reactions from Janna when she started charting a unique course for herself as a teenager.

Janna's struggle to understand Nancy's actions took years of soul-searching—both individually and together. The notion that the twinship is a sacred place is a forceful deterrent to a quest for self. How ironic that what actually served to solidify and validate their twinship was when Janna and Nancy became comfortable with themselves as individuals.

Alignment

For twins working on "self" is a foreign concept. Nonetheless, twins must find a way to work on themselves as individuals before they can heal whatever wounds may exist in their twinship. To do this, twins must venture beyond the safety of the twin relationship (at least emotionally) and spend time concentrating on themselves as individuals.

Singletons can relate to the desire to find their own identity. However, it would be more difficult for them to empathize with the battle of attempting to face life as an individual apart from your twin. This predicament hits the very core of twinship. As a twin, it is easy to focus on your twin, or even your twinship, to avoid taking a good hard look at yourself. While it is true that many people assume the role of "victim" and desperately seek someone else to blame for their troubles, this game is much more convenient for twins—you only have to look in front of your nose. Transfer of blame to your twin or twinship is almost effortless.

Nancy and Janna began to recognize this pattern of projection in their lives once they reunited in San Diego. They had a huge "a-ha" moment when they realized that one contributing factor to this problem centered around unrealistic expectations. Janna expected Nancy to follow her lead. Nancy assumed that Janna's words were always judgmental. It took great courage to break this habit. They acknowledged that their expectations were outdated leftovers from childhood. Old tapes of how each other used to react needed to be erased and replaced with new behaviors—like not having expectations! They needed to learn how to react differently than they had in the past.

Go ahead, just try to act differently in a situation that pushes one of your well-worn buttons! For instance, if you have a tendency to curse at other drivers on the freeway, tomorrow try smiling instead. It will definitely feel uncomfortable at first, but it will make your day more pleasant. Rather than having your day ruined by someone who is completely beyond your control, your day will be made better by someone who is under your control—YOU! Keep practicing reacting differently and eventually it will feel so good to feel good that you will stop re-acting, and simply act.

None of this will happen overnight. Nancy and Janna have worked on their twinship, and consequently themselves, for years. Evolution has been necessarily slow and deliberate. The lessons of their childhood twinship were forgotten in their busy adult lives. They forgot to stay balanced, both inside and outside of their twinship.

Staying with the idea of keeping life simple, let's break each person down into four essential parts: the physical self, the emotional self, the mental self, and the spiritual self. These parts are similar to four tires on a car. If one tire goes flat, everything is out of kilter. On the other hand, if one is too full, the car is equally off-balance.

Janna and Nancy have discovered that paying attention to and nurturing each of these pieces helps them to be whole persons. Emotional needs are met through loving contact with family and friends; physical needs are nourished by following a healthy lifestyle, both in food choices and regular exercise; mental needs are fostered through reading, seminars, and work (this one seems to be the easiest to take care of); and spiritual needs are infused by relaxation, daily meditation, seeking, and studying. You can stabilize yourself in as many different ways as there are people on the planet, but the bottom line is: go ahead and do it!

Once individuals feel comfortable and whole, their relationships will follow suit. Relationships also have the four components that need attention. The two (or more) people who are involved must take the time to develop these parts. Someone once said, "Home is not the place to come to when you are tired of being nice." Bring a whole, actualized, happy person home and project that person into your relationships. You will see a difference.

Balance and individuality came hand-in-hand to Nancy and Janna. They found that staying aligned as individuals has made their twinship a better place to be. This vision of their relationship is vividly symbolized by the words of Fran Dancing Feather at the beginning of this chapter.

THROUGH THE EYES OF ANIMALS

Although it is true that hindsight is 20/20, Janna and Nancy were amazed at how Fran could see straight to the heart of them. Reflecting back on their lives through the eyes of Eagle and Buffalo, Nancy and Janna see a clearer picture of themselves.

Eagle and Buffalo are a lot like twins. They exhibit opposite traits, just as twins tend to do. Eagle is of the sky, Buffalo is of the earth. Eagle is far-sighted, flying high overhead searching for prey; Buffalo is near-sighted, roaming to find food right under his nose. Eagle is sleek and majestic. Though strong, Buffalo is really quite cumbersome and homely.

It is paradoxical that Nancy, the beautiful Eagle, felt so inadequate when cast in the part of Dumbo the Elephant. Interestingly, their roles in these second-grade plays were perfect portrayals of the side of each of them that Janna and Nancy needed to nurture and develop. Nancy needed to treasure that part of Dumbo that represented stability and family, while Janna needed to love that part of Cinderella that was sponta-neous and unafraid of risk.

Eagle Woman

Like Eagle, Nancy had an insatiable wanderlust to fly from the twinship, spreading her wings to explore and conquer the unknown. She took a thousand-foot view of life—unable to focus on the details. This behavior was a source of great frustration for Janna as Buffalo.

Nancy was not the least bit interested in family matters. Besides spending Sunday afternoons watch-ing football with the family, she did not enjoy family time. The truth was that those Sundays were part of Nancy's life only because she loved football, not because she was drawn to the comfort of the family circle.

Unlike Buffalo, Nancy valued her friends more than her family. She took family for granted with the attitude that no matter what she did, her family would love and forgive her. As with Eagle, you simply could not cage her free will. When she committed a transgression, she was undaunted by standard forms of punishment. Nancy would either detach her feelings or crack a joke to relieve the tension. As a result, it was difficult to ever really punish her. Nancy's mother tells many stories of laughing so hard that she was unable to follow through with discipline, no matter how egregious the offense. Nancy had a way of just flying away from conflict.

This happy-go-lucky attitude is part of Nancy's personality. After she graduated from college, she moved back to her parents' home. Oh, how Nancy loved the freedom of being an adult living "at home." She interpreted it as having no responsibility—like her childhood days. Alas, this free ride was short-lived.

Within the first month of this precarious living arrangement, her mom and step-father insisted that she move out. It seems that the revolving door of friends who came and went at all hours of the day and night, making themselves welcome to food and drink, were even too much for Nancy's delightful sense of humor to mask. The folks were finally able to stop laughing long enough to give Nancy the big boot. Though the parting was angry, in no time, as predictable, all was forgiven. Eagle's free spirit—Dancin' Nanc—had won again.

Buffalo Woman

In direct contrast, Janna, like Buffalo, was very grounded and stable. She was immersed in the small details of life—often referred to by her sisters as "Mom's Conscience." Janna was a professional worrier. She worried about Nancy, their wardrobe, their checkbook, their car, their social calendar, while Nancy stood away calmly detached from the emotion of their lives.

Janna was not only Nancy's caregiver, she served that function for the rest of the family as well. This duty became more obvious as she grew older. Janna's buffalo-like strength became a leaning post for the family. Her many hours logged in on telephone calls with all the family members attest to the extent to which the family looked to her for wise counsel.

As they were a family of five women, Janna stepped to the plate as family fashion consultant. She graciously armed herself with the curling iron and hairspray to make sure all the ladies had an acceptable "do" for a family evening out. No one bothered asking her if she wanted to provide these favors. It was her assumed role. Buffalo does not complain about her weight of responsibilities.

Ironically, Janna's strength is offset by great sensitivity. This trait makes her a good provider, like Buffalo.

However, for Janna, it turned into a sacrifice of her own needs for those of others. From wearing her heart on her sleeve to feeling Nancy's pain, Janna was a bundle of emotions, always on the verge of bursting. Her expression of these feelings ranged from quiet tears of disappointment to thundering screams of anger.

When Janna was in her early twenties, the weight of the responsibility for both her own and Nancy's feelings became too much to bear. The endless burning inside was a fire she could not put out. A long overdue trip to the doctor revealed the source of the flame: a duodenal ulcer.

In looking for a tidy solution to the problem, Janna asked, "What do I have to stop eating to make the pain go away?" The doctor astutely responded, "The ulcer isn't caused by what you are eating, but rather by what's eating you."

This reasoning made sense, but sadly, Buffalo knew no other way.

Touched by the Earth, Kissed by the Sky

Even though these animals epitomize Janna and Nancy, their domains are equally meaningful to these twins. The separate roles (Nancy being sky-bound and Janna being earth-bound) could not provide all they needed to be whole within and without their twinship. It is never enough for twins to settle into their roles as opposites and abandon the other side of themselves.

Nancy had to realize that Eagle desired the earth to live fully. Eagle's nest, her home base, is fabricated on and of the earth. Nancy had to learn stability from Janna so that she could keep her feet on the ground and her head out of the clouds. She had to stop taking her family, and especially Janna, for granted. Nancy has made great progress, but has not yet fully integrated earthliness into her flights of fancy.

On the other hand, Janna, as Buffalo, had to focus her vision beyond the life-giving earth so near to her. Buffalo had to appreciate the bounty of the sky which brings rain to the parched fields. This gratitude assures that more rain will come another day. Janna had to learn openness and bountifulness from Nancy so that she could free her trapped joy and let go of fear.

Eagle and Buffalo are complete when they weave Earth and Sky into their lives to accomplish the partnership that makes all things possible. Together Wolf is born.

Teachings of Wolf

Wolf represents the best of Eagle and Buffalo. Like Buffalo, she would sacrifice herself for her family. Like Eagle, her vision is vast and she owns great territory.

Wolf is very intelligent: knowing how to master all kinds of weather, carefully stalking her prey, tenderly caring for her family, and lovingly mating for life. She teaches all she knows to her pups, passing down traditions to help ensure survival.

Yet, Wolf reluctantly understands the necessity of solitude. At times she ventures away from the pack to judge the lay of the land. Her discomfort with this task is echoed by her deep howls of loneliness as she sings her longing to reconnect with her family. When the anticipated reunion occurs, the celebration is marked with the dance of play.

Wolf is both serious and silly. Wolf has spoken to Nancy and Janna to introduce them to the need to blend traits in their lives. Nancy has had to temper the clown in herself with the acceptance of responsibility. Janna has had to loosen her composed self with an occasional naked jig in front of the refrigerator.

Fran told them that they are Wolf together—the Great Teacher. This description confirmed for them that this book was the fulfillment of part of their dual purpose. Through her teachings, Wolf blessed Nancy and Janna with an awareness to share what they have learned as twins and as individuals. They sincerely hope that you can see beyond the lessons for twins to the lessons for every man and every woman.

APPENDIX I:  TWIN MAP

Identical Twins	**Fraternal Twins**
Walt and John Born: 5/9/59 Arnhem, Holland	Vince and Andrea Born: 9/30/65 Kansas City, Missouri
Cindy and Wendy Born: 3/19/55 Los Angeles, California	Karen and Sharon Born: 2/23/61 San Diego, California
Karen and Kathy Born: 11/17/58 Blue Bell, Pennsylvania	Vivian and Helen Born: 10/14/05 San Antonio, Texas
Besse and Esther Born: 8/5/17 Vancouver, BC, Canada	Joy and Jennifer Born: 1/3/53 Evansville, Indiana
Fran and Josephine Born: 4/17/36 Newark, New Jersey	Suzanne and Rich Born: 10/13/67 San Diego, California
Chris and Cathy Born: 9/22/56 Santa Fe, New Mexico	Shari and Kari Born: 5/10/52 Bainbridge Island, WA
Rhonda and Renee Born: 2/13/67 San Antonio, Texas	Graham and Janet Born: 10/27/56 Lancashire, England

Continued . . .

Identical Twins

Earl and Gearl
Born: 11/17/33
Stanton, Texas

Darlene and Arlene
Born: 5/18/49
Ontario, Canada

Gina and Tina
Born: 8/26/62
San Diego, California

Nancy and Janna
Born: 5/5/57
Amarillo, Texas

APPENDIX II

THE TWIN BOND

Tips for Nontwins

Accept the twin bond—it is forever
- Do not put your twin friend in a situation of having to choose between you and his/her twin

Give your twin friend the gift of time to be with his/her twin

Do not attempt to compete with your friend's twin
- Nurture your own relationship with your friend apart from the twin

Develop your own relationship with your friend's twin
- Show interest in the twin, not jealousy

Honestly discuss with your twin friend your feelings about the exclusionary nature of the twin bond and its impact on you

Remember twins' propensity for sharing and high tolerance for closeness

Spend time with the twins together: be a student of the relationship that the twins have with each other in order to gain insight into your friend's relationship skills

Tips for Twins

Remember that others cannot substitute for your twin
– Do not seek a twin replacement outside the twinship
– Be aware of moving too quickly in relationships

Honor and nourish your twinship as the special relationship that it is
– Unconditional trust is unique to your twinship

Learn to be alone, not lonely, by giving yourself space from the twinship

Appreciate that others have a need for alone time and space

Develop friendships outside the twinship

Spend time with your twin discussing aspects of your twinship and the effect of it on other relationships

TIPS ON BEING
A POSITIVE EXTERNAL FORCE

Use a physical trait to tell twins apart
- If there is not an obvious trait, create a distinction for small children, such as a bracelet for one or part their hair on different sides

Most of the time use a given name, not "Twin" (or "The Twins") to address twins
- Twins can correct you if you are wrong
- Parents can encourage twins to correct name mistakes

Take time to know the twins separately
- Respect them as individuals

Dress twins alike, but be sensible
- Vary it—buy mix-and-match clothes
- Let twins have a choice when they are young
- Dress them alike sometimes for the fun of it

Give different gifts that fit the individual personality of each twin (consider each twin's interests, hobbies, and traits when choosing a gift)

Do not compare and categorize the twins
– Recognize and acknowledge individuality

Please do not stare, gawk, or point; just go ahead and ask

TWINSPEAK

Tips for Nontwins

Do not get in the middle of a twin battle or a twin hug
– When your twin friend wants to vent about his/her twin, listen without judgment and do not criticize the twin

Appreciate that twins are accustomed to nonverbal communication; be patient and verbalize your feelings

Talk openly and often with your twin friend about communication styles

Any feelings or issues you have about your friend's twin should be communicated directly to that person (do not try to convey messages by going through your friend)

Do not assume your friend's twin is the same person as

your friend; look for unique personality traits

Tips for Twins

Learn to use words to express your feelings at the time you have the feelings

Be sensitive to the impact of the twin zone on others

When you are with your twin and your significant other, remember to acknowledge your significant other

Reassure your twin that your significant other is not a replacement for him/her

Do not expect others to react like your twin does

Talk to your significant other before making plans with your twin
 - Be considerate of your significant other's agenda in your life

YIN AND YANG BALANCE

Tips for Twins

Recognize who is dominant and who is passive; discuss whether those roles are still working in your twinship

Examine your behaviors outside the twinship; answer the question: Who am I when I'm not with my twin?
– If you are not the same people inside and outside your twinship, discuss if that is acceptable or work on balancing it

Recognize that each of you have all the traits—you are not half a person without your twin

Do not look to your twin to fulfill all your needs

Do not insist that your twin satisfy your expectations for his/her life
– Do not try to "run" your twin's life

Keep evaluating your twinship over the years

SEPARATION

Tips for Parents of Twins on Separating Twins in School

Generally, letting twins be together for as long as possible is the best approach, but be aware of the personalities of your twins and make separation decisions with them in mind
- Is one twin more accelerated academically?
- Is one twin more dependent?
- Do they distract each other or help each other?
- How much time have they spent apart before the first day of school?

Consider what is best for them, not what the school officials think
- Let the twins have input in separation decisions

Watch carefully how the twins handle the separation; if they exhibit trauma, it's probably too early to split them up

Tips for Twins on Psychological Separation

Take an honest look at your twinship
- Is one of you more dependent on it than the other one? (Do you ever over-identify yourself as a twin?)

- Does one of you feel stifled by the twinship or resentful of it?
- Are you tired of the roles you set for yourselves in childhood?
- Do you argue more often than not?
- Do you feel like running away from each other, but feel too loyal to the twinship for that?

If you see any pattern of dependency (and co-dependency), you probably need to separate yourselves from the twinship
- Recognize old tapes and erase them
- Examine old wounds and release them
- Spend only quality time together
- Communicate your need for space to your twin
- Practice switching roles with each other to see how it feels

IF THE BOND BREAKS

Tips for Twins

Get together and discuss your relationship (not just superficially!)

Analyze your roles in the twinship and check to see if they still fit or if they need to be redefined

Shine the light on that warehouse of boxed issues; discuss them, forgive them, and forget them; let go of the past.

Set boundaries
- What is an acceptable level of advice between the two of you?
- What do you want from each other?
- How often are you comfortable seeing or speaking to each other?
- What were your childhood roles and are you still playing them? Is that okay with both of you?

Examine your twinship in relation to your relationship with your significant other
- Deal with any jealousy issues
- Try to all be friends (or at least respectful of one another)
- All three of you work together to identify the problems and solutions
- Don't let your significant other replace your twin in your life

Understand the meaning of co-dependency; make sure you are handling it in your twinship

Being a twin is a gift; don't give it away lightly

SUGGESTED READING

We suggest the following books for your journey of self-discovery. Some are directly related to twins, but all will touch you.

1. *Codependent No More: How to Stop Controlling Others and Start Caring for Yourself* by Melody Beattie.

2. *The Celestial Bar* by Tom Youngholm.

3. *The Celestine Prophecy* by James Redfield.

4. *Don't Sweat the Small Stuff . . . and It's All Small Stuff* by Richard Carlson.

5. *I Am Enough* by Margaret Storz.

6. *Illusions: The Adventures of a Reluctant Messiah* by Richard Bach.

7. *The Measure of Our Days* by Jerome Groopman.

8. *A Prayer for Owen Meany* by John Irving.

9. *The Psychology of Twinship* by Ricardo Ainslie.

10. *Revolution from Within* by Gloria Steinhem.

11. *The Seven Spiritual Laws of Success* by Deepak Chopra.

12. *The Silent Twins* by Marjorie Wallace.

13. *Travels* by Michael Crichton.

14. *Your Erroneous Zones* by Wayne Dyer.

15. *You'll See It When You Believe It* by Wayne Dyer.

About the Authors

Nancy J. Sipes earned her doctorate degree in molecular and cellular biology, and has worked passionately in the biotechnology field for the last ten years. Her love of writing shifted her career into a writing partnership with Janna. She lives and writes in the trusted sunshine of San Diego, California, where she shares her home with her husband, Stu, and their two dogs, Eddie and Lola.

Janna S. Sipes has spent the last decade in the challenging field of law practicing in various roles, from litigator to in-house counsel, in both Texas and California. Her favorite role in life has been that of being a twin, thus writing with Nancy is doubly rewarding. Janna also lives in sunny San Diego, only minutes away from Nancy and Stu, with her canine friends, Ozzie and Search.

Not surprisingly, Nancy and Janna share their passions for hiking (they ascended Mt. Kilimanjaro in 1997), meditation, long strolls on the beach, and watching sports.

To contact the authors, write to **Twinergy Works**, 4735 Clairemont Drive, #287, San Diego, CA 92117; e-mail: < twnsipes@san.rr.com >.